Beginner's Guide to
Rose Growing

Black Spot. Infected Leaves

Mildew. Showing leaves, stem and receptacle badly affected

Rust on Rose Leaves

CYRIL C. HARRIS

Beginner's Guide to Rose Growing

DRAKE PUBLISHERS INC

NEW YORK

Published in 1972 *by*
DRAKE PUBLISHERS INC
381 *Park Avenue South, New York,* N.Y. 10016

Printed in England

ISBN 87749–142–9

Library of Congress Catalog Card Number 75–175962

Contents

Illustrations

Both Author and Publisher wish to thank the following for
permission to use the photographs as indicated:
The Murphy Chemical Company Ltd, frontispiece; Mon. J.
Poyet, Societe des Produits Mais, France, No. 1; Samuel McGredy
and Son Ltd, Nos. 3, 4, 6, 7, 8, 13, 14, 15, 16; R. Harkness and Sons
Ltd.; Nos. 2, 5, 9; Fisons Pest Control, Nos. 10, 11; J. Stubbs Esq.,
Ph.D., B.Sc., Plant Protection Ltd. No. 12; *The Field Newspaper*,
No. 17.

DRAWINGS

CHAPTER ONE

Introduction

There have been many changes in our mode of living in the past twenty-five years. These have been mainly created by various economic factors that did not exist in pre-war days. Some of them have had bad influences, whilst others have had beneficial ones. Of these changes, there is no doubt that the ones that have affected gardens and gardening practices are those that have caused it to become fashionable nowadays to have small gardens. This situation has mainly stemmed from two causes.

Firstly, for some years there has been a severe shortage of building land, partly due to the rapid exhaustion of supplies of suitable plots, and partly due to the very much stricter official regulation of the use of any sites that become available in order to preserve amenities. As a result there has been a fantastic rise in the cost of building land in Great Britain, which has made it imperative to utilise any plots that come on to the market as economically as possible. Many old houses with large gardens have either been divided into several or demolished, and numerous new homes have been constructed in their grounds. Even owners of houses with more modest gardens have been tempted by the high gains to be obtained and the opportunity to reduce their commitments to dispose of a portion of their land so that several residences occupy the space that originally accommodated only one.

The second factor that has had a great influence on gardening in the last twenty years is the shortage and high cost of labour. In the first place, the old-time professional gardener as we once knew him, has largely died out. In the second, in pre-war days unfortunately there was a large number of unemployed who were only too happy to lend a helping hand in return for a very modest sum, usually lower than the rate for the job, to eke out their comparatively low unemployment pay. Happily in these days, no such assistance is available. Consequently in the majority of cases the maintenance of the garden falls upon the shoulders of the house-owner, sometimes with the help of his wife, or vice versa.

The advent of small gardens and the scarcity of labour has brought about a considerable amount of re-thinking on gardening and planting during the past fifteen or twenty years. The great shortage of professional gardeners has inspired the introduction of a spate of mechanical aids, more especially designed for the use of 'weekend' gardeners. Selective weedkillers have been developed so that the tedium of weeding by hand has been almost completely eliminated. Many of the very lovely features of the old-time gardens have almost become memories of the past. The herbaceous border and annual bedding out, for example, were early victims of these changing circumstances. Many of the rather rank-growing trees and shrubs, so popular formerly, have fallen out of use because there is no longer room for them. The thoughts of garden planners have turned to the more compact-growing types of plants that in former days only found a place in the forward positions of borders. The restricted amount of room available has given rise to a demand for plants that not only occupy a small area, but that also well earn their keep by blooming more than once throughout the summer – a characteristic that is known to horticulturalists as 'remontancy'. It is no longer possible to follow completely the practice of our forebears of planting a large variety of plants that maintain continuous massed colour in the garden by flowering in succession as the summer passes.

It is against this current background, that this book deals with roses and endeavours to describe how the traditional ideas of roses in gardens must be changed if they are still to be enjoyed. As with other plants, roses, which during these years of change have maintained their great popularity, have been called upon to meet these new conditions. This has in fact been done in the face of adversities, because, as incredible as it may seem, during this same period, very marked alterations have taken place in the nature and qualities of these plants. These changes have unfortunately made it harder for them to fit in with these new gardening conditions. The difficulty has been largely brought about by indisputable fact that while gardens have been becoming smaller, our modern roses have become larger. Many present-day roses are characterised by a great vigour that makes them grow easily to a height of 4 feet 6 inches. They are far greater in size than most of the bedding roses that were grown before the war. Many of them are in fact so strong growing that they are unsuitable for planting in the traditional way in the many small gardens of today.

This marked change in roses in this respect dates from 1948, when Peace, perhaps the loveliest of hybrid tea roses, was introduced. This variety proved itself to be one of the most vigorous hybrid tea roses known up to that time. It probably owes much of its strength to the very old species rose, *Rosa foetida bicolor*, which features late in its pedigree. This rose itself is a sport of the species, *Rosa foetida*, which is known to have existed as early as the sixteenth century. The latter reaches a height of 10 feet or more, with ease, when growing in the indifferent soil of Persia, where it originated. Furthermore, because of its great popularity, hybridists have used Peace continuously as a parent of many of our present-day roses. It is doubtful whether any other rose can boast of as many progeny as it can. Many of its descendants have inherited the great vigour of their famous ancestors. Thus, the reason can be seen why it is so difficult for many of our present-day roses to fit comfortably into the smaller modern gardens that exist in this country today. In consequence there has to be quite a lot of re-thinking on how they can be effectively used. Already, in many instances the traditional ideas have had to be abandoned and new planting schemes devised in order that the new roses can still be enjoyed in their more restricted surroundings. It is one of the objects of this book to deal with this aspect of modern gardening and to make suggestions as to how roses can be incorporated into garden plans applicable to small gardens.

There is no doubt that the disappearance of the professional gardener has forced upon amateurs, often with a degree of welcome, the need to know more about the reasons for doing certain gardening operations. It is therefore the intention to endeavour to meet this need in these chapters, as far as it is possible. It is proposed to go to some extent beyond ordinary gardening methods and to provide as much information as possible relating to the modern research and development work, affecting cultivation and maintenance, that has been carried out in recent years.

To begin with, the influence of Peace and its forebears is not confined to the production of vigorous roses. It has also had a profound effect on the methods of pruning modern roses. These are appreciably different from the traditional techniques and have, in fact, led to considerable controversy among gardeners. Both Peace and *Rosa foetida* dislike being cut back hard and often show their resentment, if so treated, by flowering sparsely in the following summer. This quality they have handed down to their many progeny. In consequence it has now been conceded by enlightened rose experts that there is a real change in the make-up of many of our modern hybrid tea roses, compared with those of 30 years ago, and that if the best results are to be obtained, new pruning techniques are necessary (page 92).

Another great controversy that has raged in gardening circles on the question of pruning is the time during the winter or spring when they should be pruned. This has been the subject of some quite heated argument among gardeners. So great have been the differences of opinion on this subject that much confusion has arisen in the minds of many amateurs, particularly those who are beginners. In a later chapter in this book, this is one of the subjects that it is hoped to elucidate (page 91).

In addition to pruning, there are other aspects of cultivation and maintenance that have more recently come under review. Later, an attempt will be made to describe some of these in greater detail and give the reasons for the conclusions that have been reached on them. For example, there was a time, when it was claimed that clay soil was absolutely essential to the well-being of roses. Sometimes one still finds a gardener who believes that this is true. In a large garden, perhaps the choice of a part, where the soil is of this nature is possible, or perhaps in the days of cheap labour it could be economically brought in, but in a present-day small garden, it is necessary to use anything that is available, if it is desired to grow roses. Current knowledge dictates that almost any soil, even a chalky one, can be rendered in such a way that roses will flourish in it.

Even the question of how rose beds should be dug has become the subject of some discussion. Although there are still some adherents living, who insist that double digging is an essential to good rose cultivation, it is now conceded by most gardening experts that the manner in which a bed should be treated depends upon the nature of the soil. Under some circumstances, digging one spit deep is quite satisfactory (page 54).

Possibly it is in the field of fighting insect pests and diseases that the greatest advances have been made during the past twenty years. It is thought that it is in this respect that modern amateur gardeners can benefit by being given a greater understanding of the pests, bacteria and fungi that cause the damage and a knowledge of the nature of the chemicals that are currently used for controlling them. Considerable progress has been made particularly in the field of insecticides. Almost every pest known can be destroyed or controlled on most plants by spraying with the appropriate chemical. Among the most important advances is the discovery of systemic insecticides, which are absorbed by the leaves and stems so that when the sap-sucking and the leaf-eating insects attack a rose they are poisoned. In addition to their being effective, they are also labour-saving because the frequency of spraying is substantially reduced when compared with the older contact type of insecticides.

Unfortunately the progress in these modern insecticides has brought in its wake misfortune to the harmless forms of wild life that abound in our countryside and gardens. Indiscriminate spraying, both on the large and small scale, has caused in recent times considerable misgiving among many people. The outcry against it has been so great that scientists have been inspired to devise research programmes designed to discover selective insecticides that are specific in their action against the destructive pests only and to develop other methods of eradicating them without harming other forms of life. This is very important and a fascinating subject and, although a knowledge of it is not essential to the growing of good roses, it is felt that numbers of discriminating gardeners would wish to have some information on the more recent approaches that are being made. A little space is therefore devoted later on in this book to dealing briefly with this question (page 137).

Turning to the equally distressing subject of rose diseases, the more common of these are caused by fungi. Although behind the scenes considerable advances have been made in our knowledge of their nature, the fungi that cause them and the reactions of the host plants, we still appear to be some way off the discovery of a panacea that can eradicate these diseases entirely. Over the years, a series of chemicals have been found that appear to be successively better, and no doubt one will be discovered eventually that is able to prevent and cure the various fungus diseases that affect roses. The alternative approach to the eradication of them, that has been made by scientists, is to breed types and varieties, that are not susceptible to attack. In recent years there has been a great demand from gardeners for hybridists to turn their attention to this aspect. Horticultural scientists have by no means neglected this side of the problem. In fact, very considerable work has already been done, particularly in the United States, with this aim in view. Achieving this object however, is inevitably a slow process.

To date research workers have not got very much beyond com-
pleting the preliminary work that is essential to the setting up of a
full scale programme designed to breed roses immune from disease.
It must be admitted that it might be quite a long time before the
desired results are obtained, but the signs are not without hope. A
lot of very interesting work has however, been done and a large
amount of knowledge has been accumulated on the nature of the
various types of roses, the characteristics of the diseases and that of
the fungi causing them and the pathological effect that they have on
the plant themselves. This is such an important subject that it is
thought that it would be of interest to rose gardeners to have some
knowledge of the approaches that horticulturalists and scientists are
making to this problem. For this reason it is discussed at greater
length in a subsequent chapter (page 149).

The importance of recurrent flowering in the small garden has
already been mentioned. Considerable attention has been given to
it by breeders of modern roses during the past twenty years because
it is realised it is an essential factor in the maintenance of colour
over long periods in a restricted space. Throughout this book
particular emphasis will be given to this aspect of rose growing.
One very important example, that might be mentioned at this
point is the group of hybrid tea-type floribunda roses, that give
lovely clusters of hybrid tea-type blooms, often as great in size as
the flowers of hybrid tea roses. Being relatively compact they are
able to give a good measure of colour in a comparatively small space.
They are, in fact, dual purpose roses, combining the delightful
spray effect of the traditional floribundas with the beauty of the
perfect, high-centred, shapely hybrid tea blooms. So important have
these varieties become to small garden-owners that a considerable
number of experiments have been carried out in order to determine
the best way of pruning them so as to impart to them this much
sought-after quality of recurrent flowering (page 98). The second
important example of types of roses that have been bred with
remontant properties are the modern *kordesii* climbers, which have
the enormous advantages over the old-time ramblers and climbers
of being compact, modest growers that bloom repeatedly, and of
requiring little or no pruning or tying up.

While it is hoped that experienced rose growers will regard this
book as something of a treatise in which an attempt has been made
to give an account of the modern developments in roses and their

uses in modern gardens, every endeavour has been made to provide all gardeners, particularly beginners, with an up to date guide to the growing of high quality roses. With this aim in view the layout of the text has been arranged in such a way that the more academic discussions can be skipped initially by those who are primarily interested in practical details. Perhaps later, they will have more inclination to study them and will return to the pages that they have at first passed over and read at their leisure something of the exciting story of the painstaking endeavours that are being made by scientists and hybridists throughout the world to create the perfect rose.

CHAPTER TWO

Older Ways of Using Roses

As time passes, there are fewer people who recall the expansive gardens of former days, where it was possible to have sweeping lawns that took two, or perhaps more, under-gardeners several days of each week to cut laboriously with razor-sharp hand-mowers, resulting in what had the appearance of a vast billiard table. These lawns were perhaps bounded on two sides by flowering shrubs, conifers and other ornamental trees that had over the ages grown so densely together that it was almost impossible to see the bare earth beneath them. Behind them, at predetermined intervals, grew the larger forest trees, such as copper beech, the Canadian maple, horse chestnut, the American scarlet oak, *Magnolia grandiflora ferruginea* and many others that can only be grown in wide open spaces, all giving the most glorious colours, blending with those of their smaller companions set at their feet and the brilliance of the green of the newly cut grass. Elsewhere, there would be found the glorious spectacle of a grass walk through a pair of the loveliest colour-laden herbaceous borders, which were not lacking for one moment during the whole season, any of the many tints that their occupants could so generously provide.

Wandering aimlessly through such a garden, one would unexpectedly stumble on features, each of which, at their time of season, came into their own and provided a blaze of colour. In one corner, where perhaps the subsoil was chalky, or lime had been purposely laid down, there would be found a compound of the most glorious irises, ranging in colour from the blue of the common flag to perhaps the exquisite medley of orchid-pink, raspberry red and tangerine, or equally fantastic hues, flourished by some more recently introduced variety. Then, at the further end of the lawn, there would be another secluded area possibly hidden from view by a shrubbery, devoted to a formally laid out garden of paeonies, or as an alternative, it could be a tulip garden. Once their short flowering period is over these various formal gardens could be forgotten by their affluent owners and left to themselves and the administrations of the under-gardeners to regain their strength so that they could once again give forth their best a year later.

Perhaps the most expansive and glorious of all the formal gardens to be found in these extensive grounds was devoted to roses. As befits a family of plants that does not let up in blooming from the beginning of June, or earlier, until Christmas Day, the space devoted to them was often greater than that allowed to any other flower. The rose garden was often almost a sanctuary, surrounded by a high brick wall or a yew hedge, so old that it had attained a width of no less than six feet, so sharply clipped that it might have been done by a myriad of gardeners each wielding a razor blade. The entrance to this space was usually one of great majesty – perhaps it was marked by a pair of the most delicately fashioned wrought iron gates, bearing in gilt the coat of arms of the owner. Within, the paths between the many symetrically-placed, geometri- cally-shaped beds could be made of lovely weather-worn York stone, or, equally as charming, closely cut grass or even colourful loose stone chippings.

The centre of this glorious garden might be dominated by the most elegant statue, perhaps enlivened by water sparkling in the sunshine, falling vigorously into a formal pool below. The main centre pathways were perhaps demarcated by substantial pergolas, possibly constructed in brick or weathered stone and seasoned oak timbers. The secondary paths might be lined on either side with oak posts between which were draped stout ropes. It would be difficult to determine with ease the nature of the material from which these structures had been constructed because they would have been closely covered with climbing roses and ramblers in such a way that the roses became an architectural feature of the garden. If the master of the house was a frequent visitor to France, he might have been influenced by the effects produced by the methodical French gardeners at the rose gardens at Bagatelle or at the Roseraie de l'Haÿ in Paris and have insisted upon his servants faithfully reproducing their artistry.

There could be many other features in this marvellous garden of the past, the entrance to a minor part of it might be marked by a rustic or trellis arch. Where height was required, pillars or pyramids might rise out of the ground, and there might be weeping rose trees symmetrically placed in strategic positions. Whatever the structures might be they would be always clothed in the carefully

trained shoots of ramblers and climbing roses. All the favourites –
some very old indeed – would be among them, mentioning at
random but few, there could be pale cream Félicité et Perpétue,
pale pink to white Mme. Alfred Carrière, the fragrant Dr W. Van
Fleet with its lovely pale pink flowers, crimson purple Veilchenblau, the immortal rose-pink Dorothy Perkins and so many more.

Below this high structure would be seen a multiplicity of beds, all
rigidly geometrical in shape and symmetrically sited so that as a
whole they form a most strict formal pattern. In some gardens, this
formality would be emphasised by edging each bed with dwarf
box-edging, all most meticulously trimmed to give it the sharpest
of outlines. These beds would be packed with a most marvellous
collection of hybrid tea and hybrid perpetual roses – each bed
being always devoted to one variety – and so arranged that an
observer would see a harmonious mass of colour growing at the feet
of the pillars, tripods, pergolas, arches and so on that carry the
equally colourful climbers overhead. If it were possible for a
present-day rose enthusiast to visit one of these rose gardens today,
the first thing that would strike him, after he recovered from the
overwhelming glorious effect of the ensemble, perhaps rather
mundanely, would be how low-growing all these bush roses are –
mostly not higher than his knees. How unlike the vigorous specimens that we have in these days!

Although this conception of the old-time rose garden is a figment
of imagination, fortunately there are places where this grandeur can
still be seen. Most of these gardens are open to the public and are
well worth a visit. Among them are Luton Hoo, Queen Mary's
Rose Garden in Regent's Park, Kew Gardens, Polesden Lacey in
Surrey and further afield, but perhaps the most exquisite of all,
Bagatelle and Roseraie de l'Haÿ in France. In any of these, a
glimpse of the glories of the past can be obtained.

CHAPTER THREE

Modern Ways of Using Roses — 1

In the last chapter an attempt was made to paint a word picture of a rose garden of former times. For the purpose of emphasis the one described was rather grandiose, but even a more modest one would be quite elaborate and contain features that would be very difficult to fit into a small garden of today.

Perhaps before proceeding further, it is important for the reader to have some idea of what is intended in this text to be the definition of a small garden because the terms 'large' and 'small' are relative ones. It is thought that a plot with a total of about ⅕ of an acre, (50 feet × 160 feet), that provides, in addition, the space for a house or bungalow, garage and drive-in, might be reasonably regarded as the upper limit of size for a small garden. In most such hereditaments, the front and back gardens are separate entities, only linked by a fairly narrow strip of land. Thus, there are two areas, one, say 50 feet × 30 feet in the front and another possibly 50 feet × 110 feet, in the rear, which have to be planned. It is realised that such spaces must sound fabulous to the owners of modern town houses, who still want to grow roses. They will be glad to know that their needs are dealt with in a later chapter (p. 182). It is very important to remember that the figure of ⅕ of an acre that has been defined as the area of a small plot is the upper limit. It is fully realised that there are many keen gardeners who have appreciably smaller ones. The requirement of owners of such gardens are certainly kept very much in mind in the ensuing chapters.

Incidentally, ⅕ of an acre is the area of my own site. In this garden I grow nearly 150 roses. To many people this sounds quite a lot, and they imagine that with such a small area they would find roses dominating the scene. But such is not the case, because by careful planning it has been possible to absorb them into this space, together with over twenty conifers, more than 50 dwarf and large azaleas and rhododendrons, something like 150 heathers, including three tree heathers, one of which *Erica lusitanica*, is a magnificent plant, growing at least 10 feet high, and a host of the smaller

21

shrubs and foliage plants. This garden has been developed over the past ten years and has given considerable experience, which is not only of value in dealing with a garden of this size, but also with ones that are appreciably smaller.

In Chapter 1 reference has already been made to the possibility that the great vigour and tallness of many of our present-day roses has been derived from Peace, that figures in the pedigrees of a very large number of them. Also it was suggested that this rose, in its turn, is likely to have inherited its own great strength from one of its own forebears, *Rosa foetida bicolor*, which is known to have existed at some date prior to 1590, when it was thrown as a sport by another very ancient species rose, *Rosa foetida* (also known as *Rosa lutea*). These are certainly very categorical statements to make and do call for some justification. In the first place, nobody can deny that Peace is a parent or an ancestor of a very large number of hybrid tea roses. Any reader, taking the trouble to sit down and patiently look at the Royal National Rose Society's book *Roses—A Selected List of Varieties* and a number of this year's rose-growers' catalogues containing the current new introductions, would find it very easy to pinpoint 100 or more modern roses that can claim to have among their parents, grandparents or great-grandparents this miraculous hydrid tea rose, Peace. No doubt there are others, because there are sure to be some of the earlier progeny that have become obsolete. This reader would also find that the majority of these roses that he has picked out are either described as being 'vigorous, tall and upright' or 'vigorous, tall and branching'. Only here and there, would any roses be found that are described as moderately vigorous or of medium or compact growth. With such evidence in its favour, it is difficult not to come to the conclusion that Peace has a good deal of responsibility for the fact that so many modern roses are vigorous and tall in growth.

On the other hand it has to be admitted that there are also some roses of today, which show no evidence of the presence of Peace in the later stages of their pedigrees and that despite this they are equally as vigorous and tall as those that have. Among these, might be mentioned buttercup-yellow Buccaneer, golden-yellow Golden Giant, Liberty Bell, whose petals are claret rose with light cream on the reverse side, bright pink Margaret, Mojave, which is deep orange and reddish flame, silvery pink Monique, deep salmon-red Montezuma, white Pascali, brilliant orange-red Soraya and

Teenager, the blooms of which are rose-pink in colour, shading to yellow at the base with cream reverse. It might therefore be argued on this basis that the suggestion that Peace or its forebear, *Rosa foetida bicolor* is responsible for the vigour of our present-day hybrid tea roses is inaccurate, but it must be remembered that in drawing attention to the above exceptions that only the last one or two generations of parents have been checked. Possibly a more comprehensive study might show that *Rosa foetida* or its many others of derivatives are well-established in their ancestry, and also in that of many others of the tall growing roses, that cannot claim Peace as a forebear.

Another important point that should be noted is that five out of the ten roses named above have colours ranging from brilliant yellow to brilliant orange-red. This might be a very significant point because it was such colours as these that the French breeder, Pernet Ducher, introduced for the first time some seventy years ago into the world of roses. At this time, starting with *Rosa foetida persiana* the 'Persian Yellow', yet another sport of *Rosa foetida*, he created in three generations of crossing the first non-fading golden-yellow rose 'Soleil d'Or, ever known. This rose was the forerunner of the brilliant yellows, scarlets, flames, oranges and bicolours that grace our rose beds today. So it is possible that there is something of the *Rosa foetida* blood in those roses in the above list that have colours in this range. To establish all these conjectures with certainty would entail a considerable amount of very interesting research, but it would of course take quite a lot of time.

So far this discussion on the possible cause of the great vigour in our roses today has been confined to hybrid tea roses. In view of the great popularity of floribunda roses in these days, it is of interest to see whether they have been effected in the same way. Perhaps it is a remarkable thing, but the great majority of this type of rose, which some years ago were regarded as more robust than the hybrid teas, grow in a more modest fashion than their counterparts. Of course, the origin and the line of descent of the floribundas are distinctly different from those of the present-day hybrid tea roses. An examination of their pedigree reveals that the presence of Peace or *Rosa foetida* and its derivative is far less frequent than it is in the case of the hybrid teas. There are, however, some modern floribundas that have Peace among their ancestors, but not in every case does this produce the vigour and height that it seems to do in the case of the hybrid teas. Quite a number are described as being 'vigorous, growing to a medium height,' suggesting that the tall-growing factor has been suppressed by some other characteristic.

Examples of this type of floribunda are cherry red and yellow Happy Event, orange-yellow Innisfree, orange-salmon Irish Mist, Paddy McGredy, with its carmine blooms, which incidentally is quite a modest grower, rich cerise Pantomime, Redgold, Shepherdess, the flowers of which are yellow, flushed pale salmon and deep salmon to carmine coloured Tombola. On the other hand, there are a few descendants of Peace among the floribundas, such as pink and silver bicolour Daily Sketch, Red Dandy and Sea Pearl, the flowers of which are pale orange and pink, with yellow reverse, that are described, like the hybrid tea roses with similar pedigrees, as being 'vigorous, tall, branching (or upright)'. This could be confirmation of Peace having the ability to impart this tall-growing quality to its progeny.

There is another factor that has probably contributed quite materially to the preponderance of tall, vigorous cultivars among our present-day roses, which is more economic than genetic. There is no doubt that when Peace was introduced just after the end of the Second World War it was hailed by the gardening public as a miracle rose and it became tremendously popular. This popularity is shown by the fact that over 30,000,000 bushes have been sold and, even now, nearly 30 years after its birth, it is still a good seller. It could be that its popularity at the time was boosted by the fantastic tale of how it was created during World War II, escaped from occupied France in the United States diplomatic bag, and how it was sensationally re-christened 'Peace' – it was originally named 'Mme A. Meilland' – at the close of hostilities. Whatever was the reason for its great popularity, the fact remains that it sparked off a demand from gardeners for more and more roses like it.

This encouraged breeders to produce a number of such roses using Peace as one of the parents. After all, rose hybridists are in business to make a profit and they cannot be blamed for accepting the doctrine that 'the customer is always right'. Unfortunately subsequent events brought about the changed conditions in the garden already described, and the fickle-minded public are nowadays tending to demand lower-growing hybrid tea roses that are more adequate to their smaller gardens. In fact, as unfair as it might be, there is an inclination to blame rose-hybridists for the fact that so many of the very beautiful varieties available are so strong and tall-growing. Unfortunately to bring about this change is not just one of simple re-tooling, and it might take up to a decade to put the breeding trend into reverse.

In chapter 2, an attempt has been made to give readers an impression of the splendour of an old time formal rose garden. While many of its features are not possible in our present-day gardens, some of them can be quite effectively translated to them – perhaps in a rather more modest style. It cannot be denied that to plant hybrid tea roses in formal beds is one of the loveliest ways of displaying them. It is not now always possible to segregate a part of the garden and devote it solely to roses in the way it was done in former days, but it is feasible to find an existing area that lends itself to a formal arrangement. This can often be in close proximity to the house. It could, for example, be a terrace bounded at its rear by the wall of the house and a straight retaining wall on its further side.

Another part of a small garden that has a formal air is the front garden, which is usually rectangular in shape and is crossed by straight paths and a drive in. As well as formal rose beds, this might accommodate along its front boundary or the drive, climbing roses neatly trained on posts and hanging ropes. Carefully placed standards and one or two weeping rose trees might not be out of place.

In a long and narrow garden, the lower portion might make an excellent site for a formal rose garden. To form this, an area should be separated from the rest, by planting a hedge across the garden at a point about $\frac{2}{3}$ of its length from the house. In the middle of it there should be left a gap to give access to the part beyond. In order to recapture at least a little of the atmosphere of the beautiful rose gardens of former days, this hedge might be of closely clipped yew. If the garden can be enclosed on all four sides by a hedge of this sort then the setting for roses would be perfect. Yew, however is expensive and slow growing. For such gardeners who would like an alternative, a good second choice is *Lonicera nitida*.

Beyond this hedge, geometrically-shaped beds are cut in the lawn to form an overall formal pattern. The actual shape of the beds is determined by that of the centre one. Two typical designs are given in the diagrams on page 26. These beds should be separated by

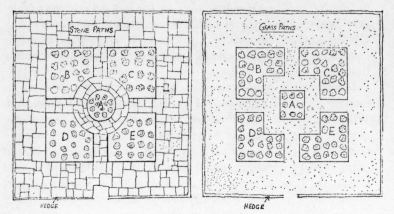

FIG. 1. *Two Formal Layouts of Roses*

closely mown grass paths, which, if it is in proportion to the total area, should not be less than 4 feet wide. Alternatively, they could be laid in York stone, either crazy or random rectangular. If this material is used, the formal scene might be enhanced by placing a statuette in the middle of the centre bed.

It is now necessary to say a few words about the not too easy task of finding shorter-growing roses for such a small scale rose garden. Perhaps the first most important rule, that must be obeyed, is that they should be uniform in height. To some extent this is helped by planting out each bed with the same variety. It is asserted by some that formal beds should only be filled with hybrid tea roses, but with the advent of the floribunda-hybrid tea type, which has hybrid tea-shaped flowers growing in clusters, it is hard to see that it really matters in these days. In any case, it is generally easier to find now-a-days shorter-growing trees among the floribundas than the hybrid tea roses. Even if one adheres to the former view, floribundas of the hybrid tea type could be very effectively used in the middle bed. There are a number of combinations that might be used, but the following is put forward as an attractive suggestion (see Fig. 1 above):

Bed A   King's Ransom or the floribunda Goldgleam (Yellow)
Bed B   Champ Elysées (Deep velvety crimson)
Bed C   Virgo (White)

Bed D   Miss Ireland (Coral salmon and yellow)
Bed E   Picture (Clear pink)

Another attractive way of growing roses formally in a small garden
is on a rose walk, which might, for example, be the link between
the front and rear gardens at the side of the house. If the beds are
backed by a fence or the house, this will afford the opportunity of
growing some of the very lovely taller modern hybrid teas as a
background. I once visited a cottage that stood originally alongside
a disused gravel drive, which ran between its back and a 4-feet-high
bank. The distance between them was about 16 feet. When the
present owner restored the cottage, he had the drive taken up and
replaced with bought-in soil. Down the centre he laid a grass path
about 6 feet 6 inches wide leading to a paved courtyard at the
further end of the cottage. The beds flanking it were planted with
roses. The whole effect was very beautiful and a magnificent reward
for the very hard work that its construction entailed.

There are, however, some small owners of small gardens who are
unable to find space enough for a formal garden of the sort described.
How can they have the great pleasure of growing roses? This
question leads to the suggestion that some re-thinking must be done
on the manner in which roses must be grown to meet the demands
of modern gardening. It has already been stated that many of the
most beautiful present-day roses grow too vigorously and too tall to
give satisfaction under the conditions that exist today. The best
solution to this problem is to grant to hybrid tea and floribunda
roses their rightful place in the garden as shrubs and to grow them
in shrub borders, where they can mingle with the other occupants
and give brilliance of colour in summer at a time when many
shrubs are rather on the dull side.

Furthermore if roses are to be successfully incorporated into small
gardens, it is necessary to take a broader point of view regarding
them than has been hitherto taken. There is a great tendency at
present to consider hybrid teas, floribundas and, to lesser degree,
the modern climbing and shrub roses as the full quota available.

The thoughts of gardeners should embrace to a greater extent the
rose family as a whole because its members are so versatile. Among its
many members there can be found a wide variety of types, habits,
sizes, colours and perfumes. In the case of size alone, for example,
at one extreme it includes the species *Rosa omeiensis pteracantha*, that

grows to a height of 15 feet, while at the other, there is the charming miniature Mon Petit, that rarely exceeds 5 inches. Between these two limits, there is a wide range of roses that can meet almost any need in the garden. They include, among others, the species roses, modern shrub roses, floribundas, floribundas-hybrid tea type, dwarf floribundas, hybrid teas, polyantha pompons, recurrent flowering climbers and ramblers and miniature roses. From this array of several thousands, it is easy to make a selection that can satisfy all desires.

It is certainly much easier to make a choice of suitable roses for growing among shrubs in small gardens than when they are needed for formal beds because the taller hybrid teas, such as buttercup-yellow Buccaneer, that grows to a height of 6 feet, can be easily accommodated towards the back of the border. For a long time there has been a school of thought that maintained that hybrid tea roses are only suitable for formal beds and that, if any roses are allowed to enter the shrubbery, they should be confined to the floribundas. It is doubtful whether this is still valid nowadays because it is difficult to conceive a more beautiful sight than Peace in full bloom flanked by a variety of shrubs. In any case in a small garden, it is difficult to think in what other position it can be so easily enjoyed. It might be a wrong conception, but it almost seems as if Nature has anticipated the needs of the twentieth century by producing quite a number of types of roses that are eminently suitable for present conditions. It has already been pointed out that often hybrid teas cannot be really satisfactorily grown because of their height and vigour, but the pleasure of having them can still be enjoyed by planting in shrub borders and other suitable positions, floribunda-hybrid tea type, the first of which, Fashion, was introduced by Eugene Boerner in 1947. They have the delightful characteristic of growing large clusters of hybrid tea-like roses. She has also created a very wonderful hybrid tea rose, Pink Favourite, that, if disbudded, grows the most superb exhibition blooms, but when left to go its own way produces large clusters of flowers. Whichever way it is treated, it is an excellent subject for the shrubbery.

In more recent years, a number of shrub roses have been introduced. They rarely grow higher than 5 feet. Some, such as apricot, shaded pink Grand Master, yields clusters of very lovely semi-double blooms that are reminiscent of those of floribundas in shape. Others give flowers not unlike hybrid tea roses, such as those of

Golden Showers, which, although classed as a large flowered climber, it rarely exceeds 5 feet in height, and can be grown as a free shrub. Turning to the less vigorous members of the rose family, the poly-antha pompons, which have been rather neglected in more recent years, rarely grow higher than 2 feet and are excellent for forward positions in the border. They produce the most delicate sprays of flowers, all most delightfully coloured in varying shades of red, vermilion, yellow, pink, salmon pink and white. Another very valuable group of roses for this purpose are the dwarf floribundas, which are an especially short-growing group of floribundas. They only reach 15 inches in height. Perhaps the most spectacular of them is Baby Masquerade, which has blooms that are exact replicas of the larger version, Masquerade. Still smaller are the miniature roses, some of which have blooms that are bijou images of the hybrid tea roses. They have a very beautiful range of colours (see page 35). Together with the dwarf floribundas, they make excellent ground cover.

Roses are very easy to incorporate in a shrubbery border because there is very little colour competition with the shrubs. Often when among tall shrubs they are excellent planted in groups of four or six, so that they give a mass of colour. On the other hand, if the need is to give height to low-growing plants and to provide colour in that part of the garden, when they are out of flower, often one rose bush can produce a very satisfactory effect. Recently I was very impressed with the way roses were used in a fairly small bed that was flanked by a York stone crazy path, and had at its rear a very lovely bush of *Hebe* × Midsummer Beauty, the spreading habit of which made it stretch almost the whole length of the bed. In front of it were planted some fairly tall growing floribunda roses, Evelyn Fison and Faust, with dwarf azaleas, a silver variegated dwarf shrub *Euonymus fortunei gracilis*, and *Erica carnea Startler* growing at their feet. In late June, the effect of the vivid red Evelyn Fison and the golden yellow, tinged with pink, of Faust against the background of the lavender blue spikes of the Hebe, with the massed green of the ground cover plants below, was just superb.

In the following pages are given some tables of various types of roses that are suitable for the various purposes described in this chapter. In order to assist the planning of them in formal gardens and shrubberies, an endeavour has been made to indicate the relative heights to which they grow. It will be appreciated that this is a difficult thing to do with any precision because it is likely to vary according to the conditions under which they are grown. In the tables, in the case of hybrid tea and floribunda roses it is assumed that their average height is 3 feet and this is indicated as 'medium'.

ROSES FOR MODERN GARDENS

A Selection of Hybrid Tea Roses

VARIETY	HEIGHT	VARIETY	HEIGHT
White		Grand'mère Jenny	Medium
Virgo	Short	Wisbech Gold	Medium
Pascali	Medium	Peace	Very tall
Creamy White		*Light Orange with*	
Westfield Star	Short	*Bronze Shading*	
Creamy White with		Lady Belper	Short
Yellow Shadings		*Orange Amber*	
McGredy's Ivory	Short	Apricot Silk	Medium
Blush White		Whiskey Mac	Medium
Memorium	Short	*Orange Brown*	
Royal Highness	Medium	Fantan	Medium
Buff Cream		*Orange/Yellow*	
Burnaby	Medium	Doreen	Very short
Diamond Jubilee	Medium	*Orange Yellow and*	
Elizabeth Harkness	Medium	*Deep Apricot*	
Mr Standfast	Medium	Beauté	Short
Yellow		*Orange with Gold Base,*	
Belle Blonde	Very short	*Veined and Shaded with*	
Dorothy Peach	Short	*Red and Bronze*	
Lydia	Short	Bettina	Medium
McGredy's Yellow	Short	*Orange Carmine with*	
Grandpa Dickson	Medium	*Gold Shadings*	
King's Ransom	Medium	Violinista Costa	Medium
Western Sun	Medium	*Copper/Orange*	
Golden Giant	Tall	Mrs Sam McGredy	Short
Peer Gynt	Tall	Vienna Charm	Tall
Summer Sunshine	Tall	*Ginger*	
Buccaneer	Very tall	Ginger Rogers	Tall
Cassanova	Very tall	*Pale Pink with Yellow*	
Gold Crown	Very tall	*Shades*	
Yellow Edged with Pink		Ophelia	Medium

VARIETY	HEIGHT	VARIETY	HEIGHT
Pink and Orange		Konrad Adenauer	Short
Angels Mateu	Short	Mme	
Pink/Cream		Louis Laperrière	Short
Honey Favourite	Medium	Papa Meilland	Short
Salmon Pink		Alec's Red	Medium
Femina	Medium	Brilliant	Medium
Mischief	Medium	Ena Harkness	Medium
Santa Fé	Medium	Ernest H. Morse	Medium
Deep Pink Striped		Marjorie Proops	Medium
with White and Light		Milord	Medium
Pink		John S. Armstrong	Tall
Candy Stripe	Tall	Red Devil	Tall
Pink		*Vermilion*	
The Doctor	Short	Duke of Windsor	Short
Ballet	Medium	Fritz Thiedemann	Short
Bond St.	Medium	Fandango	Medium
Charm of Paris	Medium	Fragrant Cloud	Medium
Evensong	Medium	Fragrant Charm	Medium
Guinevere	Medium	Isobella de France	Medium
Pink Favourite	Medium	Olé	Medium
Prima Ballerina	Medium	Montezuma	Tall
Princess Paola	Medium	Super Star	Tall
Shannon	Medium	*Blue/Lilac*	
Lady Seton	Tall	Prelude	Short
Percy Thrower	Tall	Sterling Silver	Short
Eden Rose	Tall	Blue Moon	Medium
Cerise Pink		Cologne Carnival	Medium
Mullard Jubilee	Short	Godfrey Winn	Medium
Carmine Shaded		Heure Mauve	Medium
Orange Salmon		Lilac Time	Medium
Shot Silk	Short	Silver Star	Medium
Cerise flushed Carmine		*Bicolours	
Wendy Cussons	Tall	*Pink/Cream*	
Coral Red/Yellow		Gail Borden	Medium
Anvil Sparks	Very short	My Choice	Medium
Red		Stella	Medium
Champs Elysées	Short		

Bicolours are roses with blooms that have distinctly different colours on the inside and on the outside of their petals respectively.

VARIETY	HEIGHT	VARIETY	HEIGHT
Pink/Silver		Cleopatra	Very short
Adair Roche	Medium	Tzigane	Short
Gavotte	Medium	*Scarlet to Yellow*	
Isobel de Ortiz	Tall	*at base/Yellow*	
Rose Gaujard	Tall	Piccadilly	Short
Orange Salmon/		*Orange Scarlet/Yellow*	
Yellow		Gay Crusader	Medium
Colour Wonder	Medium	*Vivid Scarlet/Silvery*	
Coral Salmon/Yellow		*Pink*	
Miss Ireland	Short	Grand Gala	Tall
Red/Yellow			

A Selection of Floribunda Roses

VARIETY	HEIGHT	VARIETY	HEIGHT
White		Goldilocks	Short
Garnette White	Very short	Kerry Gold	Short
Ice White	Medium	Norris Pratt	Medium
Iceberg	Very tall	Summer Meeting	Medium
White with a Lemon		Yellow Cushion	Medium
Tinge		Arthur Bell	Tall
White Spray	Medium	Geisha Girl	Tall
Creamy White		Golden Treasure	Tall
Grace Abounding	Medium	Honeymoon	Tall
Matterhorn	Tall	*Golden Yellow*	
Cream/Amber/Pink		*shaded Crimson*	
Sweet Repose	Medium	Angela	Medium
Cream overlaid Peach-		*Yellow with Pink*	
pink		*shading*	
Chanelle	Medium	Circus	Medium
Cream flushed with		*Yellow/Pink/Red*	
Yellow and Pink		Baby Masquerade	Dwarf
Columbine	Medium	Masquerade	Medium
Yellow		*Gold with Orange Tips*	
Garnette Yellow	Very short	Manx Queen	Medium
Adeline Genée	Short	*Apricot Yellow*	
Allgold	Short	Sir Lancelot	Medium
Goldgleam	Short	*Apricot edged and*	
Golden Jewel	Short	*flushed with Crimson*	

VARIETY	HEIGHT	VARIETY	HEIGHT
Alison Wheatcroft	Medium	Sleepy	Dwarf
Apricot Orange		Garnette Carol	Short
Joyfulness	Medium	Garnette Pink Frills	Short
Coppery Yellow		Garnette Rose	Short
Copper Delight	Very short	August Seebauer	Medium
Summer Song	Very short	Charlotte Elizabeth	Medium
Orange shading to		Herself	Medium
Yellow		Pink Parfait	Medium
Zambra	Very short	Vera Dalton	Medium
Orange		Queen Elizabeth	Very tall
Garnette Orange	Very short	*Cerise*	
Orange Salmon		Susan	Short
Bobbie Lucas	Medium	*Carmine Pink*	
Irish Mist	Medium	Paddy McGredy	Short
Jiminy Cricket	Medium	*Red*	
John Church	Medium	Grumpy	Dwarf
City of Leeds	Tall	Happy	Dwarf
Salmon shaded Gold		Garnette Red	Very short
Tombola	Medium	Marlena	Very short
Salmon Pink		Radar	Very short
Garnette Salmon		Sarabande	Very short
Pink	Very short	Ama	Short
Margo Koster	Very short	Red Favourite	Short
Petite	Very short	Rodeo	Short
Pernille Poulsen	Short	Satchmo	Short
Salmon Sprite	Short	Sir Galahad	Short
Tip Top	Short	Dr Barnado	Medium
Border Coral	Medium	Europeana	Medium
Dearest	Medium	Highlight	Medium
Elizabeth of Glamis	Medium	Korona	Medium
Mrs Richards	Medium	Lilli Marlene	Medium
Patricia Hyde	Medium	Red Dandy	Medium
Rose of Tralee	Medium	Santa Maria	Medium
King Arthur	Tall	Fear Naught	Tall
Scented Air	Tall	Fervid	Tall
Pink		Ohlala	Tall
Bashful	Dwarf	*Vermilion*	
Doc	Dwarf	Meteor	Very short
Jean Mermoz	Dwarf	Excalibur	Short

VARIETY	HEIGHT	VARIETY	HEIGHT
		BICOLOURS	
Orange Sensation	Short	*Peach and Biscuit/*	
Anna Wheatcroft	Medium	*Yellow*	
Evelyn Fison	Medium	Violet Carson	Medium
Orangeade	Medium	*Salmon Pink/Silver*	
Arabian Nights	Tall	Celebration	Medium
Dorothy Wheatcroft	Tall	*Pink/Silver*	
Glengarry	Tall	Daily Sketch	Tall
Scarlet Queen		*Pale Orange and*	
Elizabeth	Tall	*Pink/Yellow*	
Blue/Lilac		Sea Pearl	Tall
Africa Star	Short	*Orange Red/Old Gold*	
Maud Cole	Short	Attraction	Medium
Lake Como	Short	*Orange/Golden Yellow*	
Lilac Charm	Short	Golden Slippers	Very short
News	Short	*Vermilion Orange/*	
Silver Charm	Medium	*Yellow*	
Blue Diamond	Medium	Fresco	Medium
Escapade	Medium	*Scarlet/Silvery White*	
Magenta	Tall	Molly McGredy	Medium

A SELECTION OF POLYANTHA POMPONS

Unless otherwise indicated the average height is 15 inches

COLOUR	VARIETY
Crimson	Eblouissant
Pink	Ellen Poulsen
Coral Pink	Coral Cluster
Coral Salmon	Little Dorrit
Salmon	Cameo
	(Taller than average)
Golden Salmon	Golden Salmon Supérieure
	(Taller than average)
Orange Scarlet	Gloire du Midi
	(Taller than average)
	Gloria Mundi
	Paul Crampel

A Selection of Miniature Roses

Their average height is 12 inches.   Any deviations are indicated

VARIETY	HEIGHT	VARIETY	HEIGHT
White		Cricri	Average
Princesita	Average	Eleanor	Average
Creamy White		*Pale Pink*	
Pour Toi	10 inches	Rosemarin	Average
Blush White		*Pink*	
Cinderella	Average	Humpty Dumpty	6 inches
Pixie (Little Princess)	9 inches	Perla de Monserrat	Average
Yellow		Rosa roulettii	Average
Baby Gold Star	Average	Sweet Fairy	8 inches
Bit O'Sunshine	Average	Twinkles (Shading	
Pixie Gold	Average	to white)	5 inches
Rosina (Josephine		*Red*	
Wheatcroft; Yellow		Coralin	Average
Sweetheart)	18 inches	Maid Marion (Mon	
Yellow Doll	9 inches	Tresor, Red Imp)	10 inches
Orange Pink		Mon Petit	5 inches
Little Flirt	Average	Robin	18 inches
New Penny	Average	Scarlet Pimpernel	Average
Apricot Shaded Orange		*Blue/Lilac*	
Colibri	Average	Baby Faurax	Average
Salmon		Purple Elf	6–8 inches

A Selection of Modern Shrub Roses

VARIETY	HEIGHT
Cream flushed Pink	
Penelope	4 feet
Yellow	
Golden Wings	5 feet
Buff Yellow	
Buff Beauty	4 feet
Apricot Yellow	
Grand Master	4 feet
Salmon Pink	
Felicia (Shaded yellow)	4 feet
Nymphenburg (with yellow base)	6 feet

VARIETY	HEIGHT
Red	
Elmshorn	5 feet
Heidelberg	6 feet
Kassel	5–6 feet
Prestige	6 feet
Uncle Walter	6 feet
Vermilion	
Bonn	5 feet
Fred Loads	5 feet
Scarlet Yellow	
First Choice	4–6 feet
Lavender Pink	
Lavender Lassie	4–6 feet

A Selection of Species and Old Shrub Roses

VARIETY	HEIGHT
White	
Blanc Double de Coubert (*Rugosa*)	4 feet
Mme Hardy (Damascena)	5 feet
Yellow	
Canary Bird (*R. xanthina spontanea*) (Blooms in May)	5 feet
Pink	
Cécile Brunner	2–3 feet
Frau Dagmar Hastrup (Rugosa) (Frau Dagmar Hartopp)	4 feet
Striped Crimson and White	
Rosa Mundi (*R. gallica versicolor*)	4 feet
Crimson Purple	
Tuscany (*R. gallica* shrub)	4 feet
Cardinal de Richelieu (*R. gallica* shrub)	4 feet
Mrs Antony Waterer (*R. rugosa* shrub)	4 feet

A Selection of Dual-Purpose Roses

These are hybrid tea roses that have a great propensity to bloom in clusters, but which, if disbudded, yield good specimen blooms. Because of this quality they are excellent for planting in a shrub border and in small gardens.

COLOUR	VARIETY
Yellow	Spek's Yellow
Pink/Cream	Honey Favourite
Pink/Silver	Gavotte
Pink	Pink Favourite
Red	Fragrant Cloud
Vermilion	Super Star, Montezuma

CHAPTER FOUR

Modern Ways of Using Roses — 2

In Chapter 2, when a description was given of the old-time rose garden, mention was made in some detail of the elaborate and very beautiful manner in which climbing roses and ramblers were employed. It is obvious that such methods are mainly inappropriate to smaller gardens, but this does not mean that they are entirely ruled out. They have in fact a very important role to play. The small gardens of today naturally mean that the amount of ground space is curtailed, when compared with those of former days, but despite this there are still a large number of plants that gardeners wish to enjoy. One of the ways in which this can be done is to take advantage of the relatively high amount of vertical space that is available in any garden. In this respect, climbing roses and ramblers can make a very material contribution to modern gardening.

Before discussing the various ways in which this can be done in greater detail, it might be as well to describe the differences between climbing roses and ramblers. The latter are mainly hybrids of the species, *Rosa wichuraiana*. These are known as true ramblers. There is in addition a rather lesser number that stem from *Rosa multiflora*. Whichever they are, they are characterised by flowering in clusters and doing so for a comparatively short period each season. The climbing roses include almost every other garden rose that climbs. Among these are found Large Flowering Climbers, which are roses that have been bred as such, the newer climbers that descend from *Rosa kordesii* and the well-established climbing sports of the hybrid teas and floribundas. This subject is later dealt with again in Chapter 9, in which it will be found that modern rosarians have arbitrarily classified these various climbers, according to the manner in which they have to be pruned. The modern climbers, *Rosa kordesii*, etc., are discussed in greater detail in Chapter 14.

One of the features of a small garden, which is not always appreciated is that the length of its boundaries is high in proportion to its area, when compared with a more expansive one. This characteristic is something which can be advantageously used to increase the display that can be given by roses. More usually the divisions between neighbouring gardens are wooden or wire fences, which can be effectively beautified with climbers by making use of the vertical area provided by them. It is interesting in this connection to note that in a garden, measuring 90 feet by 30 feet, which is enclosed by a 6-foot-high fence, the vertical space provided by the surrounds is slightly more than half the area of the ground available. This is indeed a good bonus for the small garden-owner. Thus, it is possible to have roses in far greater profusion than would at first appear possible. Choosing roses for such a purpose needs a certain amount of care because without it, the whole background to the garden can very soon become a sorry mess. It is useful therefore to consider for a brief moment the qualities that must be possessed by a rose to be used for this purpose. The absolute essentials for any cultivar under these circumstances is that it must be able to provide the maximum amount of colour, over the longest period of time, in the minimum of space. In other words it must be remontant, i.e. recurrent flowering. There is little room to spare for anything that has a brief, but glorious moment of blooming, after which it becomes dull and uninteresting until the next season comes round. Another important quality that a rose must possess, if it is to fulfil its usefulness to the utmost in these days, is an ability to cover itself right down to the ground with blooms and not have any lower branches that bear neither flowers nor leaves. Lastly, as is common to all other plants, the labour involved in its maintenance must be reduced to the minimum, if it is really to please the vast majority of present-day gardeners.

Having laid down the specification, let us now examine what the Rose family can offer to meet it. Speaking first of the old-time ramblers, which are so beautiful in themselves that it is a great shame to have to breath a word to their detriment, they are largely ruled out mainly by their lack of recurrent flowering and the enormous amount of labour involved in keeping them in order. Most of them flower to profusion in June for about three weeks and then never show another blossom until next year. During the summer, after flowering, they produce new shoots at an enormous rate, which means that, unless the old wood is promptly cut out and the new tied in, they become an impossible tangled mass in no time. Some types of ramblers throw their new shoots higher up the old wood, and not from the base. In consequence, their lower parts are bare.

Fortunately, almost as if nature anticipated the needs of present-day gardeners, an old rambler, Dr W. Van Fleet, gave birth in 1930 to a sport, New Dawn, which has much the same pale pink blossoms as its parent, but which is recurrent in flowering and very much less vigorous. It only grows to a height of about 8 feet. This rose is the forebear of a number of more modest growing climbers, including Bantry Bay, Coral Dawn, Parade and Pink Perpetue. Thus, with this newer type of rambler, it is possible to capture some of the beauty that the more vigorous ones imparted to the rose gardens of former days.

In the past, the climbing sports of the hybrid tea and floribunda roses, that produce blooms, that are exactly the same as their dwarf counterparts, were extensively used. At first sight, they should be ideal for growing in the vertical space provided by small gardens, but unfortunately they have, as they grow old, the disadvantage of only producing flowers and leaves at the extremities of their shoots, leaving their centre and lower parts just bare wood. This is of course a situation that is untenable in modern times, where every plant must earn its keep.

In addition to the newer less vigorous and repeat flowering ramblers that stemmed from New Dawn, fortunately there is another excellent group of climbing roses that were first introduced by the German breeder, Wilhelm Kordes, in 1940. They are often known as *kordesii* climbers. Sometimes, because they rarely grow taller than 8 feet, they are called pillar roses. They are repeat flowering and need practically no pruning or other attentions. These roses, which are ideal for the present time, are described in greater detail in Chapter 14.

Having described the possibles among the climbers, the next thing to do is to discuss the question of how climbing roses can be used most effectively. As beautiful as pergolas might be, it is very seldom that it is possible nowadays to find adequate space to erect one. The best that can usually be done is to have a line of posts, joined by a draping rope, at the back of a border, or at the end of the garden, perhaps to hide the nearby houses. If this is done, the best results are obtained by clothing it with one of the old-time rambler roses, such as pale pink, Dr W. Van Fleet or bright rosy crimson, Excelsa, because they produce long flexible shoots that are ideal for taking up the architectural shape of their supports, when they are tied in, whereas many of the more recently introduced climbers are rather too stiff to be really satisfactory for this purpose. Similarly this type of climbing rose is very suitable for covering an archway, that marks, for example, the entrance to another section of the garden. It must, however, be remembered that the maintenance of such roses is relatively high in terms of labour.

Among the most delightful way of using roses in a modern garden is to grow them on pillars. They can be used for various purposes. A number of them, for example, covered with repeat flowering climbers can very effectively give colour and height to a shrubbery. In many ways they are more suitable in this respect than standard roses because the latter always seem to be at their best in more formal surroundings. Equally as well they can function similarly in an herbaceous border in those gardens, where one still exists. Often a climbing rose triumphantly mounting a post can be used as a specimen in the lawn garden. If it is placed, for example, in the far corner of a rather small garden, it can optically give the impression of greater length, or, if densely clothed in a brightly coloured rose, such as the yellow *kordesii* climber, Leverkusen, and placed in a strategic position, it can act as an eye-catcher and direct the vision away from an unsightly object in a neighbouring garden.

Such pillars need only be rustic poles about 11 or 12 feet long, run into the ground to a depth of about 4 feet. If they can be of oak, they are longer lasting. Whatever they are, however, it is important to see that the part beneath the soil level is well-treated with a wood preservative. Sometimes the garden layout calls for something more substantial than a post, in which case a tripod might meet the case more satisfactorily. This can be constructed by running into the ground three posts, each about 12 feet long, to a depth of about three feet, at the apices of an equilateral triangle, of which the length of the sides and the angle at which the posts enter the ground are such that they meet at a height of about 8 feet above the ground. At this point they are securely strapped together. At the foot of each post, modern climbing roses, preferably each of the same variety, are planted and trained up each arm of the tripod. In a very short time, the structure will be hidden by a mass of foliage and coloured flowers.

There are occasions when something even larger is needed. It is then possible to erect a modern version of the wooden pyramid, which was formerly used so abundantly in rose gardens. In earlier days, when labour was plentiful and timber cheap, these were most elaborately constructed of lattice. Nowadays they can be simulated with old gas piping, wire and some metal pegs. Firstly, a circular bed of the desired size is cut in the lawn. The gas piping is drilled with a series of holes, equidistant around one of its ends. These holes should be of such a diameter that the wire will pass through freely. The pipe is then inserted in the ground with the drilled end uppermost, in the middle of the bed. Pegs are fixed at equal distances around the periphery of the bed. The wires are looped through the holes in the piping and run down and fixed to the pegs in the ground. On this structure can be trained climbers, forming what appears to be a miniature floral bell-tent. Suitable varieties of roses for growing on pillars, tripods and pyramids are given in the table on page 47.

There are in addition other ways in which climbing roses and ramblers can be used in the garden. They can be trained on walls, bare fences and on trellis, which might be separating one part of the garden from the rest, or concealing the odd job corner, which accommodates the bonfire, the compost heap and other essentials of good gardening. Often, with a small modern house, an outside shed is a necessity. Even the best of these is not a very pleasing sight. By training, for instance, the rambler François Juranville, with its deep fawn, pink blossoms, growing in clusters, over it, it can soon become part of the garden scene. Such an essential of modern living as a fuel tank with the aid of some trellis work can be similarly camouflaged. The loveliness of climbing roses can be enhanced by allowing them to intermingle with other climbers. There can be nothing more beautiful, for example, than the crimson red Dortmund, consorting with the rich light green leaves and large flat, white corymbs of *Hydrangea petiolaris*, or the large petunia-red blossoms, with their soft yellow stamens of Clematis Ernest Markham standing out like stars among the yellow blooms of the large flowering climber, Elegance.

So far the growing of climbing roses in the more formal way has been dealt with. This involves shaping them to conform to the architectural form of the erection on which they are trained, which involves careful and patient tying in of the shoots. There is another wilder way of growing them, which is very appropriate to modern gardens, in which the number that can be planted is restricted. This is to grow them in trees. Actually there is nothing novel about this idea because this is how some of the forerunners of our present-day roses were first seen by plant collectors. The Musk Rose (*Rosa moschata*) for instance, existed in its habitat in Asia, as a vigorous climber, reaching well up into trees, 40 feet or more in height, and *Rosa multiflora*, which is a forebear of the polyanthus pompons and the ancestor of the modern floribunda roses was discovered rambling through the branches of trees in Japan, smothering them in summer with its creamy-white blossom, saturating the air with its fruity fragrance, and illuminating them in winter with its mass of very dainty coral red fruits.

Many small gardens have at least one tree in them. In these days when houses have sometimes been built in the grounds of a larger dwelling, there could easily be a rather large dark-looking one, which is something of an eyesore, or the building site might have been an old orchard and just one apple tree, that has long given up providing fruit, has been left standing, either by accident or design. Whatever the tree is, it has possibilities as a support for a climbing rose or a rambler. By this means the ugliest of trees can be transformed into a thing of beauty.

Naturally, when choosing a climber for this use, vigour in relation to the size of its host must be taken into account. In most small gardens, it is rare to find an ornamental tree that is taller than 18–20 feet; often it is likely to be a little less. A good choice for trees reaching this height is the large flowering climber, Mme Gregoire Staechelin, which has very large loosely formed blooms, which are a gorgeous coral pink colour with crimson shading. It is very free flowering and will enliven any tree during the whole of June and July. For rather shorter trees, the less tall growing, but still vigorous rambler, Crimson Shower, is admirable. Its crimson semi-double flowers are small, but this is easily compensated by its long flowering time, which stretches from late July to mid-September. Lykkefund is another very lovely rose to be allowed to meander freely through a tree. Its flowers, which have a delicious fragrance that fills the air on summer days, are creamy yellow, tinged with salmon in colour, fading nearly to white, and grow in panicles of up to 30 blooms. Despite its lack of thorns, the lovely scented rose Zéphirine Drouhin is another excellent subject for climbing trees. It has beautiful bright carmine-pink, semi-double flowers, which cover a tree with colour right from its base to its uppermost branches, and brightens the darkest of green foliage. (See page 48.)

Another very practical way in which climbers can be enjoyed in small gardens is by not training them vertically, as already discussed, but by allowing them to grow prostrate and cover ugly objects, such as manhole covers, old decrepit walls, dry banks and stumps of dead trees that have been sawn off close to the ground. Such things occupy horizontal growing space, which can be ill-afforded in small gardens. Allowing climbing roses and ramblers to sprawl over them provides yet another means of having the pleasure that roses give. There are some gardeners, who rather similarly use these plants among low-growing herbaceous plants to strengthen the colour scheme and, of course, gain space, when it is restricted. Prostrate climbers also provide good ground cover, but to get the maximum suppression of weeds it is important to choose the more dense growing varieties. A list of roses having this quality of sprawling is given on page 48.

Already mention has been made of using rose-clad pillars to give height to a flat area or a greater sense of distance. A similar objective can be achieved by planting specimen rose bushes, standard roses and weeping roses in the lawn. Of these, it is probably better to confine the use of standard roses to more formal situations. In these days, we all rather complain about the excessive vigour and height of our modern hybrid tea roses and tend to reject them as being unsuitable for the time in which we live, but this is a way in which they can be enjoyed. How better can the beauty of tall-growing buttercup yellow Buccaneer or scarlet-coloured Uncle Walter be enjoyed than when it is planted as a specimen in a distant corner of a lawn? In a very small garden one of these might be the only rose in it, but what a glorious sight it would make in the height of summer!

Weeping standards also make very beautiful specimens in the lawn; or they might be planted in pairs to mark the entrance to another section of the garden, which might be on a higher level than the rest and be approached by steps, either made in stone or cut in the grass. Such roses are usually ramblers that have been budded on either rooted briar or rugosa stems, some five to six feet high. Of these two, the former is more satisfactory because the latter tends to produce suckers. The long shoots of the rambler, laden with colourful blossom in the summer, droop naturally down to the ground, giving a weeping effect. The rambler, Excelsa, which produces a plethora of clusters of bright rosy crimson blooms in July, grown as a weeping standard, makes an exquisite specimen.

For a smaller garden, it is possible to buy weeping standards of some of the moderately vigorous modern climbers and pillar roses, but, because of their stiffer growth, they do not fall naturally like the ramblers and have to be either tied down or trained on umbrella-shaped wire frames.

The question of the perfume of roses is discussed in greater detail in Chapter 16, but it is briefly mentioned at this point because no doubt there are some gardeners who desire to plan a perfumed rose garden. Such a layout is a particular attraction to the blind, or those with very poor sight, who derive so much pleasure from a garden through the agency of their acute sense of smell. Although it is quite common nowadays to hear people say that modern roses have lost their scent, this is not really true. There is certainly not the same proportion of them with the strong fragrance of the old Damask Rose, but most of them have some, often more unusual, perfume. This makes growing roses for their scent much more intriguing than in former days. In Chapter 16 a list of such cultivars are given.

Although I have maintained in the past that rose bushes do not by any means make the best of hedges, I think that, in view of the smaller gardens that most of us have nowadays, growing them in this way provides yet another method of enjoying them. They have a number of shortcomings as hedging plants, such as not being completely impenetrable to both humans and animals, not being evergreen and not being so amenable to trimming to a neat, crisp shape as other hedging plants. Despite this, I feel that a compromise is necessary now because of the facility that rose hedges afford to grow more roses in a restricted area. The more vigorous hybrid teas, floribundas, musk roses and the newer shrub roses, that grow four feet or over in height, are the most suitable for this purpose. They should be planted at not more than three feet apart, even less in the case of the less vigorous types. A selection of roses suitable for hedging is given on page 49.

The use of roses in the shrub border because of the colour that the flowers impart to it has already been referred to earlier in this chapter. This, however, is not all that they can contribute. Some of them, particularly the species roses, have very beautiful foliage and stem colourings, which at any time during the season can give so much interest to the shrubbery. Among others, there are the red foliage and thorns of *Rosa highdownensis* and the contrasting greyish leaves and wood of the species, *Rosa fedtschenkoana*, which can look so delightful on a sunny day, when they mingle with the light and dark greens, the greys, the golds, the reds and the variegations of the foliages of the other shrubs that occupy the shrub border. Perhaps well beyond the scope of the majority of small garden owners, because it grows to an impenetrable shrub, 15 feet high and as much across, the species *Rosa omeiensis pteracantha*, (*Rosa sericea pteracantha*), is a sight worth seeking out in late spring because its enormous thorns, an inch or more long, mounted on brown stems, glow like enormous translucent rubies, when the sunlight passes through them (See page 49).

Even after the summer has passed and the flowers fade and the leaves fall, there are other species roses that continue to enliven the bare stems of the other shrubs with their colourful hips. There seems to be no end to the variety of tints that the Rose family can provide to lighten up the foliage of the dark leafed evergreens – orange, red, yellow, purple, even black and so on are all there. In addition, they all have their own fascinating shapes. Some are round like marbles, others oval; there are bristly ones, while others are the shape of minute pears, and still others are bottle-shaped. Perhaps the most unforgettable sight is the tomato-shaped red hips, surmounted by a green top-knot of sepals, of *R. rugosa* Frau Dagmar Hastrup. A list of a selection of such roses is given on page 49.

ROSES FOR MODERN GARDENS

A Selection of Roses for Growing on Pergolas, Arches and Rope Chains

These roses are mainly ramblers because they grow long flexible shoots that are easily tied in to the shape of the object on which they are climbing. They usually only flower once a year, but it is possible to secure a certain amount of continuity of colour by planting early and late flowering varieties side by side and allowing them to intermingle. Many of them bloom in June, but those in this collection that bloom later are indicated accordingly.

COLOUR	VARIETY
White	Sanders' White Rambler
	Purity
Creamy white	Albéric Barbier
Yellow with Crimson Shading	Easlea's Golden Rambler

COLOUR	VARIETY
Deep Fawn Pink	François Juranville
Pale Pink	Dr W. Van Fleet
Coral Pink with Crimson Shading	Mme Gregoire Staechelin (June/July)
Deep Pink	Minnehaha
Rose Pink	Mary Wallace
Bright Rose (with white eye)	American Pillar (July)
Rosy Crimson	Excelsa (July)
	Crimson Shower (July to mid-September)
Bright Scarlet Crimson	Paul's Scarlet Climber
Deep Scarlet	Crimson Conquest (July)
Violet Blue (streaked with white)	Veilchenblau (July)

A Selection of Roses for Growing on Pillars, Tripods and Pyramids

COLOUR	VARIETY
White	White Cockade
Yellow	Casino
	Leverkusen
	Golden Showers
	Royal Gold
Carmine Pink	Zéphirine Drouhin
Deep Pink	Morning Jewel
	Pink Perpetue
Pink	Clair Matin
Orange-Apricot	Schoolgirl
Vermilion	Danse du Feu
Blood Red	Parkdirektor Riggers
Crimson	Hamburger Phoenix
Carmine Crimson	Parade

A Selection of Roses for Walls, Fences and Trellis

The maximum growing heights of the shorter varieties, which are more particularly suitable for covering fences, low walls and trellis work, are given. The remainder, that grow up to 15 to 20 feet high, are the best to choose for taller walls and the sides of houses.

COLOUR	VARIETY
Pale Cream	*Félicité et Perpétue
Pale Lemon Yellow	*Paul's Lemon Pillar
Pale Yellow	Elegance
Golden Yellow	Royal Gold (8 feet)
Bronze Yellow	*Maigold (11 feet)
Pink/Apricot Yellow	Meg
Coral Pink	Dream Girl (10 feet)
Pale Pink to White	Mme Alfred Carrière
	New Dawn (9 feet)
Pink	Gerbe Rose (10 feet)
Rose pink	Ritter von Barmstede (13 feet)
Bright Red	*Allen Chandler
	Copenhagen (8 feet)
	Sympathie
Vermilion	*Danse du Feu (9 feet)
Deep scarlet with darker markings	*Gruss an Teplitz (6 feet)
Scarlet Crimson	*Soldier Boy (6–8 feet)
Blood Red	Parkdirektor Riggers

A Selection of Roses that climb trees

Roses that grow in Trees up to 18 feet high	Roses that grow in Trees up to 30 feet high
White	*Creamy White*
Mme Plantier	Bobbie James
Sanders' White Rambler	Wedding Day
Rose Pink	*Creamy Yellow Tinged Salmon*
Mary Wallace	Lykkefund
Deep Pink	*Yellowish Apricot flushed with Pink*
Minnehaha	Réné André
Rosy Crimson	*Clear Pink*
Excelsa	Climbing Cécile Brunner
Parma Violet	
Rose-Marie Viaud	

A Selection of Sprawling Roses

These are varieties that, if not tied up, grow prostrate and cover
low objects. They are particularly valuable for camouflaging

* Suitable for North aspects

unsightly objects, such as manhole covers, low stumps of dead trees.
Also they can be used pegged down on dry banks and for hanging
over old ugly walls.

COLOUR	VARIETY
Creamy White	Albéric Barbier
Coppery Pink	Albertine (This rose is nearly evergreen)
Pale Salmon Pink/Yellow	Nymphenburg
Rose Pink	Ritter von Barmstede
Bright Pink	Chaplin's Pink Climber
	Max Graf
Deep Pink	Minnehaha
Rosy Crimson	Excelsa
	Crimson Shower

A Selection of Roses Suitable for Hedges

VARIETY	TYPE	COLOUR	HEIGHT
Blanc Double de Coubert	Rugosa	White	4
Chicago Peace	Hybrid Tea	Pink, base Canary Yellow	4
Cornelia	Hybrid Musk	Pink, yellow base	5
Dorothy Wheatcroft	Floribunda-Shrub	Red	4
Elmshorn	Shrub Rose	Bright Crimson	5
Felicia	Hybrid Musk	Salmon Pink, shaded Yellow	5
Kassel	Shrub Rose	Scarlet Red	6
Peace	Hybrid Tea	Yellow, edged pink	5
Penelope	Hybrid Musk	Creamy Salmon	5
Queen Elizabeth	Floribunda – H.T. Type	Pink	6
Will Scarlet	Shrub Rose	Bright Scarlet	5

A Selection of Species Roses giving Foliage and other Colour Effects in Shrub Borders and for Decorative Purposes

SPECIES	EFFECT
R. cantabrigiensis	Fern-like brownish green leaves.
R. farreri persetosa	Decorative fern-like deep green foliage

SPECIES	EFFECT
R. fedtschenkoana	Pale grey-green leaves
R. hugonis	Greyish green fern-like foliage
R. omeiensis pteracantha	Brown shoots with large ruby
(*R. sericea pteracantha*)	translucent thorns, when young
R. primula	Fern-like leaves on strong red-brown shoots, giving off the scent of incense
R. rugosa Blanc Double de Coubert	Yellow autumn tints
R. rubrifolia	Unique violet-red foliage
R. sino-wilsonii	Beautiful semi-evergreen glossy foliage
R. willmottiae	Small fern-like glaucous leaves borne on long slender plum-coloured stems

A Selection of Roses with Coloured Hips in Winter

NATURE OF HIPS	VARIETY	HEIGHT FEET
Large pear-shaped, orange	*R. macrantha* Dusterlohe	3–4
Cluster of red bottle-shaped hips	*R. moyesii* Geranium	8–10
Large deep red bottle-shaped	*R. rugosa* × Scarlet Fire	7–8
Large hairy, red, rounded	*R. pomifera duplex* ('Wolley Dod's Rose')	6–9
Scarlet fruits	*R. nitida*	2½–3
Rich red tomato-shaped hips surmounted by a green top-knot of sepals	*R. rugosa* Frau Dagmar Hastrup	3–4
Purple	*R. rubrifolia*	7–9
Small glossy red fruits	*R. rugosa* Snowsprite	3–4

CHAPTER FIVE

On Buying Roses

It is hoped that the last two chapters have emphasised the importance of deciding beforehand the purpose for which roses are required before buying. It is as well to avoid buying them on the impulse, solely because, say, their colour has a very special appeal. In these past chapters, an endeavour has been made to give general guidance regarding the types that are available and to give typical uses. At the same time, it is hoped that they have also gone some way towards shaping gardeners thoughts on modern roses. It is not possible, however, to put on paper final definitions. It is only possible to give a lead to gardeners, who must act on their own initiative and look around for themselves before making their selection. Some guidance nevertheless can be given on the steps they should take if they are to be sure of buying successfully.

Probably the first and, perhaps, most valuable advice that a would-be buyer of roses can be given is to take his time in making his final choice. Since it is not possible to plant them before October, he can, after all, take a month or two in the summer, when roses are in flower, to make up his mind. What is more, the fact that the fungus disease, blackspot, does not usually develop to any extent until late July makes it better to put off the final ordering as long as possible, consistent of course with obtaining supplies, so that there is a greater chance of finding the less susceptible cultivars, particularly among the new roses. There are a number of qualities that a gardener must consider before making his final decision so that he can be sure that any rose is going to meet his needs. Colour of course, is the quality that probably influences his choice primarily. There is only one positive way in which it can be decided that this suits his taste and this is for him to see the rose actually growing under garden conditions. While coloured prints in growers' catalogues are often very good in these days, they are not completely reliable because sometimes a picture is not quite true. Similarly descriptions in words can be inadequate particularly in the case of roses that have rather more subtle colourings. They can generally only be of value as a broad guide.

Even the very lovely displays that are set up by nurserymen at flower shows must be treated with some caution, particularly when they take place early in the year before the normal flowering season, especially when the roses are newly introduced varieties, because they will have been raised under glass. There is a chance under such circumstances that their colours will be different when they ultimately flower in the open. This could lead to disappointment.

It is also difficult to assess growing habits, vigour, proneness to disease, height of the bushes, etc., on the exhibition stand because the roses are cut flowers. It is also difficult to assess to the full these characteristics when they are inspected in the fields of a nursery. This is mainly because they are maidens, i.e. they are one year old after budding, and they are not growing under strictly normal garden conditions. Usually roses do not reach their full stature until they are a year or two older and are established in a garden. In addition it is often not possible to detect the varieties that will produce large blooms, that might be good for exhibition purposes because they are usually not disbudded. To do so would entail a large amount of labour when the roses are being grown on a large scale. Moreover, although it has little effect on the health of the plants over the comparatively short period involved, sometimes commercial growers limit the supply of nitrogen fed to them when they are maidens so that they do not produce too heavy a crop of foliage, which would mean high labour costs in defoliating them to prevent loss of evaporation during despatch. In addition, the high number of leaves left on might involve higher transport and packaging charges. It will thus be seen that such roses are not being maintained under quite normal gardening conditions and that the results might be misleading.

The most satisfactory way of choosing roses is to do so after they have been seen growing in gardens. Although this is a little time consuming, this can be done by visiting those rose growers who have demonstration gardens, in which roses are planted and maintained in the way that an amateur would do it. A close watch on the trial grounds of The Royal National Rose Society, at St Albans, Herts, is a fruitful means of keeping in touch with the new varieties that are likely to come on to the market shortly. Displays of both new and older roses can also be seen in Roath Park, Cardiff, Saughton Park, Edinburgh, Harlow Car, Harrogate (The gardens of the Northern Horticultural Society), Botanic Gardens, Southport and Vivary

Park, Taunton. In the vicinity of London, an excellent collection of all types of roses and their use on pergolas, arches, rope chains, pillars, etc., can be seen in both Queen Mary's Rose Garden in Regent Park and Kew Gardens. Another worthwhile place to visit is the Royal Horticultural Society's Gardens at Wisley, Surrey. Looking further afield, for those gardeners who spend their holidays on the Continent, superb displays of roses can be seen at the Roseraie de Haÿ and the Chateau de Bagatelle in France and the rose gardens in Madrid, Rome, Geneva, Baden Baden and The Hague. In the United States, the rose gardens of Jackson and Perkins Inc. at Newark, N.Y. are visited by many thousands of American holidaymakers every year. At Bodnant in North Wales, climbing roses can be seen picturesquely mingling with other plants.

Up to a few years ago, a considerable amount has been left to the judgement of the gardener and the guidance of his nurseryman, when buying roses, but in 1966, a valuable attempt was made to create a scientific standard of quality for roses. This was done by the British Standards Institution, when they published *British Standard 3936. Nursery Stock : Part 2 Roses.** This lays down minimum standards for bush, standard and climbing roses in terms of their age, the validity of their name, condition, i.e. freedom from diseases, pests and weeds, the degree of trimming to be carried out by the supplier before despatch and packaging. It also gives specific minimum requirements for each type, such as dimensions of the rootstock and root system, and the number and diameter and, in the case of climbers, the length of the shoots. There are a number of nurserymen who grow to this standard, which is undoubtedly a safeguard to a gardener when buying roses.

It should never be forgotten when buying that roses will probably last for 20 or more years. So it is really worthwhile going to a little trouble initially to obtain the right ones. There is no doubt that doing so will pay handsomely in the long run.

* Obtainable from British Standard Institute, 2 Park St., London, W.1.

CHAPTER SIX

Preparing Rose Beds

The questions of what is the best soil in which to grow roses and the manner in which the beds should be prepared have been the subject of keen debate for quite a number of years. Some gardeners, more particularly in the past, have staunchly maintained that they must have clay. Even today there are some stalwarts who still take this stand. It is indeed true that roses do extremely well in a clay soil, providing it has good drainage, but the principal reasons for this are that it has good moisture retention powers and it affords a cool root-run, both of which are essential to the well-being of roses.

At the same time, it has been maintained by quite a number of people knowledgeable on gardening matters that roses cannot be grown in districts where there is a preponderance of chalk. This is in fact very true, but modern techniques have shown that even the most alkaline soils can be rendered suitable for growing roses. It is an arduous task, but it can be done and is carried out by those people who must have roses in their gardens despite the chalky nature of their soil (See page 63).

Similarly, almost any other soil can be treated in such a way that it will sustain roses. Hot dry sandy soil, for example, can be mixed with copious amounts of humus material to increase its moisture-retaining powers and it can be mulched with organic substances, such as garden compost, well-rotted farm manure and grass cuttings, not only to retain the moisture, but also to keep the soil cool in hot weather. Badly water-logged heavy clay soil can be broken down to make it more friable, porous and well-drained so that roses will flourish in it and the hard labour of the gardener is diminished. To know how to condition almost any soil to suit roses is a matter of vital importance in these days because often the gardens are so small that there is no choice of position. It is largely a question of taking it or leaving it.

Even how a site intended for roses should be prepared has been in recent times the subject of much discussion. There are some who staunchly maintain that with simple digging they are able to produce roses of exhibition standard, whereas others assert that double digging, or, even trenching, is imperative. The real answer in most cases in this respect is that much depends upon the nature of the soil that is encountered. Should the bed have a heavy clay subsoil, double digging is essential to be sure that the drainage is satisfactory. Often in the case of those who maintain that double digging is utterly superfluous, it will be found in the final analysis, that they garden in light sandy, stony soil, so that it certainly presents no problems of drainage.

In the next few paragraphs, the requirements of roses, the nature of various types of soil, and the manner in which they have to be prepared are dealt with in greater detail, in the hope that gardeners will be armed with all the information they need to make their gardens suitable for growing roses, whatever their growing conditions are.

The Roots of Roses

When any plants are planted there are two main elements that have to be taken into account, when deciding how to prepare the beds in which they are to grow. The first is what sort of root system does a particular plant possess; and secondly, what kind of growing medium does it need to meet these root characteristics? Some plants, such as chrysanthemums, have all their roots concentrated near the surface of the ground. In their case, therefore, it is not necessary to dig very deeply, but it is important to provide them with a good rich, friable soil near the top through which their roots can freely ramble and absorb the nutriment that is readily available.

On the other hand, there are other plants, particularly shrubs and trees, including roses, that possess two sorts of roots. These can be seen if an established rose is dug up (See illustration on page 56). In the first place they have tap-roots which are strong and long, and grow deep down into the soil. These have two functions. They give the plant good anchorage so that it is not uprooted by strong winds, and also they search out the water in the lower layers of the soil. According to the conditions, such roots are sometimes very long indeed. With some strong-growing climbers they have been found to be as high as 15 feet in length. In any case, when a rose is dug up, it is nearly always necessary to cut through the tap-roots to release it. It will also be observed that, in addition, a rose bush has

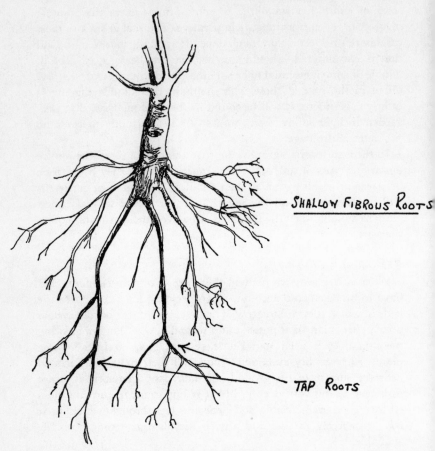

SHALLOW FIBROUS ROOTS

TAP ROOTS

FIG. 2. *Root System of the Rose*

short shallow-growing fibrous roots that have root hairs on the tips of the fibres. These grow outwards, almost horizontally, into the soil near its surface and absorb the nourishment that is available. In order that they can carry out this important task efficiently, it is imperative that there is available adequate amounts of water. It will be appreciated, when these fibrous roots are seen, that they are quite delicate. Hence it is important to be sure that rose beds are not dug deeply after the roses have been planted out, because this very valuable root system is likely to be seriously damaged.

It should be emphasised however, that although adequate moisture is important to the well-being of the plant, the ground must not be waterlogged at any time. Its drainage must be good, but the soil must be able to retain a certain amount of moisture. Another important need of a rose is to have its roots well aerated, which can only be assured in soil with good drainage because the water passing through it creates a very low vacuum behind it and this draws in the air.

From these observations of the root system of a rose, it is possible to stipulate a list of soil requirements, which should be met if rose-growing is to be successful. The fertile top soil must be friable so as to enable the delicate fibrous roots to move freely through it. It should be rich in nutriment and contain ample humus for good moisture retention. The subsoil should be of such a nature that it allows free movement of water through it and lets a good supply of air to reach the roots, and also it should be in a loose condition so that the tap-roots can easily penetrate it. Lastly, the soil should not be alkaline in its reaction, such as it would be on chalk or ground that had been previously heavily limed. It should ideally have a pH value of between 5.6 to 6.5, which is just on the acid side of neutral (See page 65).

Various Types of Soil

There are three main types of soil, other than chalky ones, that gardeners are likely to have in their gardens. They are sandy, clay and medium loam. In the ensuing paragraphs, the characteristics of each are described. Since in these days of small gardens, a gardener has little choice of soil and has to make the best of what he has got, it is very important for him to know what are the good and bad qualities of the various soils, that are likely to be available, and to understand what steps have to be taken to transform a poor soil into a good growing medium for roses.

(1) *Light Soil*

Such top soil contains a high proportion of sand. Lightness is another term for coarseness, which means that it has particles of a large size. Such soil is open and moisture passes through it easily and there is no fear of it becoming water-logged. Its main weakness is that it does not hold the water. Thus it needs the addition of

humus to increase its water retentive powers. Sometimes when the
garden is situated in heathland, light soil might contain a high
proportion of peat, which might render it rather too acid for growing
roses. This however is only likely to occur occasionally.

(2) *Heavy Soil*

This is top soil with a high content of clay. In this case, heaviness
is synonymous with fineness, i.e. it is composed of fine particles.
Because the total surface area of these smaller particles is large, clay
soil will absorb large quantities of water and become sticky; it will
not allow the free passage of water through it and there will be a
tendency for the ground to become waterlogged. It is possible to
treat it to make it more open. There are certain very satisfactory
proprietary additives on the market, but if a comparatively high
area has to be dealt with, the expense of these can be high. The
more usual way is to break down the clay with hydrated lime. This
causes the very small particles to form into conglomerates. This has
the effect of artificially increasing the particle size of the soil with
a consequent lowering of the surface area on which water can be
absorbed, making it less sticky and more porous. More water is able
to drain through it and the roots are aerated to a greater extent.
Clay soil can also be improved and made to drain more readily by
adding to it good quantities of sandy loam, leafmould, garden
compost, farmyard manure or peat.

(3) *Medium Soil (Loam)*

This is soil which is intermediate between light and heavy soil,
and is composed of sand and clay in near equal proportions. It is
the ideal soil because it has good drainage, providing it is on a
porous subsoil and it retains moisture in sufficient quantity, and
does not get sticky; but, unfortunately, there are many who are not
blessed with such soil.

Any of these three types of top soil can have a high stone content.
In some districts, it is extremely difficult to obtain stone-free soil.
Many gardeners have a rooted objection to them and embark on a
continuous process of picking stones off their beds. This is a task,
which is a pretty hopeless one because as soon as one crop is
gathered, another appears. Because of this, it is felt that it might be
worthwhile spending a few moments discussing whether stones are

deleterious or not. Unless they are fragments of chalk or soft lime-stone, there is very little likelihood of their being harmful, and, unless they are excessive in quantity, they are not detrimental to growing except in the case of some root vegetables that must be grown in relatively stone-free ground. According to British Standard 3882: 1965, which was published by the British Standards Institution in 1965, up to 20 per cent by weight of inert stony material does not interfere with normal growing. This same standard also lays down that the length, width and depth of any such stones should not exceed 2 inches.

Digging the Soil

Already it has been mentioned that a certain amount of contro-versy rages in gardening circles on what is the best method of digging the soil for rose beds. It has also been pointed out that the nature of the soil is the only criterion of how it should be dealt with. Below the principal methods of digging are described in greater detail.

(1) *Trenching*

When one talks to older gardeners, they often emphasise the great importance of trenching. In actual fact they often mean 'bastard' trenching or double digging because true trenching has rather special applications. One of the most common of these is when an unmade building plot has been taken over from a builder and he has deposited the subsoil from the footings on to the good fertile top soil. As quite a number of people move into newly-built houses in these days, this method of digging is described in detail because they might find it a help. Under such circumstances, it is necessary to bring the fertile soil, which can easily be identified by its darker colour, due to the presence of humus, to the top.

The procedure is to open up a trench 15 to 18 inches wide across the width of the plot. The top layer of rubbish and subsoil, to a depth of about 10 inches, i.e. one spit, is then dug out and placed in a wheelbarrow and taken to the further end of the plot, where it is put into a heap. The next layer, which is the fertile soil, is then removed to a similar depth and also put into a heap at the other end of the plot. The true subsoil is at the bottom of the trench and this is well broken up with a fork to provide good drainage and aeration. Next an adjoining trench of similar size is opened up by digging out the first spit of rubbish or footings and placing at the bottom of the

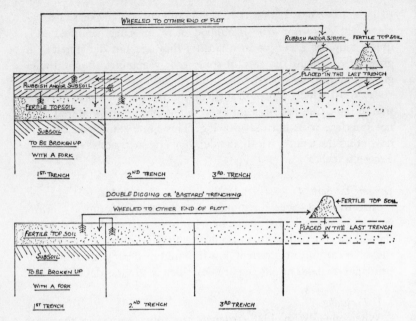

FIG. 3. *Digging Rose Beds: Trenching*

first trench; then the layer of fertile topsoil is lifted to a depth of one
spit and used to fill the trench. In the top layer of the former and
lower of the latter, humus material is incorporated in the process of
doing this. This procedure is continued in subsequent trenches right
across the bed. The last one is filled by putting in the layer of
rubbish, etc., excavated from the first trench, followed by the top
soil from the other heap. (See Fig. 3 above.)

(2) *Double Digging or 'Bastard' Trenching*

As mentioned before, true trenching is only carried out under the
special circumstances when the top layer of soil has been buried. In
most gardens it is only necessary to carry out the less arduous
process of double digging or 'bastard' trenching. By doing this, the
subsoil is broken up to make it penetrable by the tap-roots of the
plants so that they are able to search for moisture and nutrients in
the lower layers of earth and to provide good drainage. It is also
carried out to make the upper fertile layer of soil friable so that the

more delicate fibrous surface roots can readily spread out and absorb the plant foods that are essential to their well-being.

Double digging consists of opening up a trench 15–18 inches wide across the width of the bed that is being prepared. The top soil is dug out to a depth of one spit. This is carried in a wheelbarrow to the far end of the plot and heaped on to either a sack or a sheet of polythene, particularly when the bed is cut out in the lawn. The subsoil, which is now revealed, is broken up as in the case of trenching with a large fork to a depth of at least 10 inches. If the subsoil is heavy clay, the surface of it should have added to it 3 lb of hydrated lime to a square yard of the exposed area, i.e. about every 7 feet run of the trench. This helps to crumble the clay, making it more porous and thus improving the drainage. It also releases some of the nutrients, especially potassium. This is a heavy rate of liming and care must be taken to see that it is kept well down in the subsoil otherwise it will have a deleterious effect on the roses. Liming should not be done on light sandy, gravel or chalky soil.

On the surface of the broken up subsoil at the bottom of the trench, a layer of humus material should be placed. This could be chopped turves, with the grass turned downwards, leafmould, peat, containing a liberal addition of bonemeal and hoof and horn meal or rotted farmyard manure. Some humus material should be worked into the uppermost layers of the subsoil. The next step is to open an adjacent trench by transferring the top spit of it to the first. Initially, a portion of it should be added and the remaining humus should be incorporated into it. Next the rest of the top soil from the second trench should be used to fill the trench. By this action there is no risk of the roots of the roses, ultimately planted, coming in contact with any manure. The subsoil in the second trench is then forked up. The same procedure as above is followed until the last trench is reached. This is filled with the soil originally removed from the first trench. (See Fig. 3.)

(3) Simple Digging

When the soil is light and the subsoil is stony, there is no problem of drainage or tightly bound earth, through which the tap-roots might be slow in passing. It is then sufficient to dig the bed one spit deep, driving the spade vertically its full length into it and levering to loosen a block of soil, which is then lifted on the spade and turned over completely. Even with simple digging, it is an advantage to excavate the soil to the depth of a spit from a trench across the bed, set it aside and ultimately place it in the final trench. This provides a space into which each spadeful can be easily turned over. As this is being done, humus material should be dug in, but when planting eventually, care must be exercised to see that it does not touch the roots.

Drainage

Mention has already been made of the importance of good drainage – not only because roses do not like having their roots permanently steeped in water, but also because the easy passage of water through the lower layer of soil draws in air, which is required by their roots. One of the first things to do when opening up a new bed for roses is to test whether the drainage is satisfactory. This can be very simply done by digging a hole about the average size of the root system of a rose, filling it with water and allowing it to stand for a day or so. If, after this period, all the water has drained away, it can be assumed that the drainage is good. If it proves to be faulty, then special steps must be taken to remedy this defect.

This can be done in several ways. Firstly if the site is on level ground and the soil is heavy clay, it is better not to dig too deeply, but to lift the height of the beds by six to nine inches above the surrounding lawn. If the rose garden is a formal one, the soil needed to do this can be provided by having stone or gravel paths between the beds instead of grass, and using the excavated soil, that has been replaced by rubble in making them, for this purpose.

If the land has a strong tendency to become water-logged, it is necessary to introduce a more elaborate drainage scheme in the garden. It is often sufficient in such a case to dig a trench about 18 inches deep across the centre of the bed and put in about 9 inches of coarse breeze or rubble at the bottom and then to refill the remainder of the trench with some of the soil that has been excavated, making sure that the top soil is kept uppermost. Finally the bed should be raised as described above.

If complete drainage is needed, it will be necessary to dig out a series of such trenches, parallel to one another, across the site. Each should have a small downward incline towards a main trench into which it drains. The latter, in turn, should lead, once again running slightly downhill, into a sump, filled with brick rubble, situated at the lowest part of the garden. Each trench should be about 3 feet deep. At the bottom of each one should be laid agricultural pipes, with their ends touching. The latter should be covered with 12 inches of rubble and each trench filled with excavated soil.

Preparation of Rose Beds in Chalky Soil

As already stated, roses require ideally a soil with a pH value between 5.6 and 6.5, i.e. slightly acid, but actually they are very accommodating and will grow quite well, up to a certain point, outside these limits. They do not, however, like strongly alkaline conditions, such as is often found in areas with a chalk subsoil, where the pH value is in excess 7.0. This, however, does not mean that owners of gardens, that have such soil, must inevitably forego the pleasure of enjoying roses. It, however, takes quite an appreciable amount of time and patience to convert it into a suitable medium. The process is in fact a simple one in principle and consists of lowering its pH value to about 6.0. In other words, the soil has to be made more acid.

Often when a garden has a subsoil of chalk, the fertile top soil layer is shallow. The first task therefore is to remedy this defect. The most economical method of doing this is, if the ground is sloping, is to dig it up the slope. This might mean raising the site to some extent and might make it necessary to support it on one side with a low retaining wall or a bank. In most other cases, it is necessary to buy soil from an outside source. A warning should, however, be given against purchasing clay under the guise of it being good rose soil, because if the existing one in the garden is already of this type, and often chalk is associated with clay, a gardener may result in having an almost unworkable medium.

Whatever course has to be followed regarding improving the depth of soil the next step essential is to dig the soil well, throwing up as little chalk as possible. While doing this copious quantities of humus, such as garden compost, wet shredded newspapers, rag waste, leaf mould, rotted turves and grass, peat, well-rotted deep litter chicken and farmyard manure and any other material that will increase the acidity as it breaks down, should be incorporated. After this the bed is allowed to settle over the winter until the following spring, when successive crops of mustard seed should be raised. As each matures, it should be trampled down, well-watered and sprinkled generously with sulphate of ammonia. Following this it should be well dug in. Eventually soil testing (see page 65), will show that the pH value will have fallen sufficiently to allow roses to be planted. Initially it will be found to be more expedient to plant only pink and red-coloured ones because they are a little more tolerant to alkalinity than the yellows.

During the ensuing years, there may be some leaves that turn yellow. This is due to chlorosis (see page 149), and this can be remedied by watering the soil with a suspension of a chelating agent, which is sold in this country under the trade name of Sequestrene – Plus. This substance contains iron, magnesium and manganese, in a form that the plants can absorb. These elements, when in chalky soil, are often converted into a chemical form, which roses cannot assimilate. Regular additions of sulphur to the soil for several years will also ensure its maintenance at the right level of acidity.

A Suitable Site for Growing Roses

Of course before beds are prepared, it is necessary to choose a place in the garden, which roses will like. Fortunately, apart from disliking waterlogged conditions and highly alkaline soil, there are only two other things to which they really object. One is being planted in dense shade and the other growing under trees. Ideally, they like to be in a bed, in which the soil is slightly acid and well drained, which is in an open position, so that there is good air circulation, but which is shaded for some hours each day.

When marking out beds, it is always well to remember that any soil in which roses have grown for 10 or more years is likely to become what is known as 'rose sick'. This subject is dealt with in greater detail in Chapter 11, but, at this point, it is briefly explained that this means that, while old established roses will continue to do well in it, any newly planted ones, replacing any that have died, will not thrive. As will be discussed later, one of the ways of overcoming this weakness is to plant any new roses in beds in which no roses have been grown before. It is of value, therefore, in designing a new layout to make provision at the offset for being able to change the position of the beds, when necessary, without upsetting the design. This might be done, for example, by making the new ones in the position of the paths and covering the old beds with turves. By doing this, replacement can be made without difficulty, if, many years later, it becomes necessary.

Soil Testing

Although, there are no doubt numbers of readers who are interested to have a little more knowledge of the various methods used in the simple equipment sold for soil testing and the methods involved, it is not essential to have it in order to cultivate roses. Consequently any gardeners, who are primarily interested in cultivation, can quite safely, at least in the first instance, skip the remaining paragraphs of this chapter. In any case, if soil testing is necessary, it would always be possible to get it carried out by the County Horticultural Adviser and the Royal Horticultural Society for a reasonable fee.

What is pH Value?

For a long time scientists have measured acidity and alkalinity in terms of the concentration of what they call hydrogen ions in a solution. The greater this value is, the lower is the acidity of the medium, while a low one indicates high acidity. Without going into details, hydrogen ion concentration can be measured in the laboratory, using the appropriate electrical apparatus. The important thing is that it was realised many years ago that this characteristic could afford a common term for measuring both acidity and alkalinity, which had hitherto been regarded as opposites. Furthermore, it has been possible to devise a scale that covered the whole range of values representing very high acidity to very high alkalinity. This is known as the pH (potential of hydrogen) scale, on which the values have been arbitrarily set at from 0 to 14. On this, a value of 7 (pH 7) represents neutrality, while figures below this level are progressively more acid and those above indicate increasing alkalinity. This means that when a soil has a value as low as pH 4, it is very acid, whereas any values above 7 are alkaline. It should, however, be noted that a pH number of 4 is *ten* times more acid than one of 5 and *one hundred* times more so than pH 6. This is because a linear relationship does not exist between pH values and concentration of ions, i.e. when the value of the pH has doubled the actual concentration has decreased considerably more. The fundamental reason for this, which is one that will be appreciated by the mathematicians among the readers, is that there is an logarithmic relationship between these two functions.

Fortunately, the later discovery that certain dyes give constantly the same colour when they are added to a solution of the same pH

C

value has made the testing of the acidity and alkalinity of soil a very simple matter. These dyes, or indicators as they are known, act in exactly the same way as litmus paper, which turns blue to red when dipped into acid, with which everybody is familiar from their schooldays.

Soil Testing Equipment

When testing soil for any factor, it is vitally important to have a representative sample of that in the plot which is under consideration. It is therefore very important to follow very strictly the directions laid down for this purpose by the makers of the testing set being used. Normally a portion of the sample is shaken up with distilled water in a glass vessel provided in the equipment. The clear solution above the soil after settling is used for testing.

The soil testing sets available on the market consist of the very simple ones, retailing at about 2s. 6d., devised solely for checking alkalinity and acidity, medium priced sets that can be used for testing in addition the content of certain elements, which are sold at about £2, and more accurate ones, which serve much the same purpose as the former, but which cost round about £5. Anybody who wishes to be sure of obtaining good results over the full test range is well advised to purchase the higher-priced equipment.

The plant foods that can be usually measured with this relatively simple apparatus are calcium (lime requirement), nitrogen, phosphate and potassium and, in addition, of course the acidity of the soil. There are, however, some authorities, who maintain that the nitrogen content of the soil is rapidly changing from hour to hour and that no measurement made at any one time is of any value in the formulation of a forward fertilizing programme. For this reason therefore in some equipment, particularly the more expensive types, there is no provision made for determining the amount of this element in the soil.

The principle is the same in both the cheaper and more expensive sets, except in the case of the determination of potash, in which sometimes comparative turbidity is used as the basis. In all other tests, the resulting colour of the solution after the addition of an appropriate indicator or reagent is compared with a standard colour chart, which measures the content of any particular plant food. The main difference between the lower and higher-priced equipment is that in the former the colour standards are printed on cards, whereas in the latter the comparison is made against standard coloured glasses which have been calibrated against the well-known Lovibond scale of colour, and is measured in a simplified Lovibond Comparator, which is supplied with the set. The latter technique gives the more accurate results.

CHAPTER SEVEN

Planting Roses

Although it is not imperative, the best time to plant roses is in October and November. This gives them ample time to get established before the bad winter weather sets in. It is not, however, essential to carry out this work then because they can safely be planted during any period of open weather during the winter. If however, they are not planted by the third week in December, it is as well to postpone the operation until towards the end of February, when, in almost every part of the country, the severity of the winter weather is likely in a normal year to be passing away. Nevertheless, gardeners are best advised to include roses in their autumn planting programme. By this time new beds should be made and have had anything up to six weeks, in which to settle, and old rose beds, in which the occupants have grown old, will have been renovated (See Chapter 11). Also enough time would have been allowed for having a good look round, the final choice made and the requirements ordered.

One of the most important things to be remembered is that the period just before planting is one of the most critical in the whole life of a rose. It has already been mentioned that these new purchases are destined to give unending pleasure over many years—perhaps twenty years or more – so just as it is valuable to prepare the beds in which they are to lie for this long time with the utmost diligence, it is equally worthwhile bestowing on their prospective occupants the tenderest care during this period just before planting.

Giving roses a good start in their new home is a concerted effort between the seller and the buyer. Carelessness at the nursery during transit, or after they have been received by the gardener, can do irreparable damage to them. Of course, he has no control over what happens to his purchases before they come into his hands, but he can protect his interests by always dealing with a reputable rose-grower. It is always a good thing to buy the best quality roses. Although one does hear of and see plants that have been bought more cheaply as seconds that have proved to be very excellent stock, it must be remembered that they are usually being offered by an expert at this lower price because he considers that they may not make the top grade. Perhaps one of the best guarantees of receiving roses in a good condition that a buyer has in these days is the *British Standard B.S.* 3936, *Part II Roses*, which has been referred to previously, and which quite clearly indicates what can be reasonably expected from a nurseryman. Out of fairness, it must be stated that the majority of them do conform to these standards, irrespective of whether they declare that they undertake to sell to this standard.

If roses are delivered from a grower, who has failed to meet these stipulations, they must be promptly dealt with by the buyer and it is therefore of value to quote in these pages the details of those clauses in the specification that deal with these aspects. They are:—

'*Clause* (6) Plants shall be substantially free from any pest and disease, and shall be materially undamaged.

No roots shall be subjected to adverse conditions, such as prolonged exposure to drying winds or frost or subjected to waterlogging, between lifting and delivery.

Clause (7) Damaged or broken roots shall have been removed. Snags shall have been removed immediately above the union. Immature, dead and diseased growth shall have been removed. Visible suckers shall have been removed flush with the root or rootstock.

Clause (8) Packaging shall be adequate for the protection of the plants and such as to avoid heating and drying out.'

It must be agreed that none of these items is unreasonable and represents what a gardener might expect, and usually gets, from a reputable grower. Nevertheless possibly through an oversight or exceptional urgency to despatch under the threat of impending bad weather, some roses might be received that do not conform to these requirements. Then the buyer has to make a decision as to what steps to take. Certainly if they have been sold to him as complying with B.S. 3936, he is entitled to return them, but this is not always convenient and it is better for him to remedy the wrongs himself, using the above clauses as a guide. There is, however, one clause that I would expect to be met under any circumstances and this is Clause (7). Personally I would never accept roses that showed signs of having disease, because their introduction into a garden might bring something like rust, which hitherto had been non-existent in a particular district.

When, however, roses are delivered under normal weather conditions, there are two things that must be checked immediately they arrive. These are to see that the roses have been defoliated and make sure that the stems are not shrivelling. If they have not been defoliated at the nursery, and a good grower will always do this, all the leaves should be removed by cutting them off with a knife or scissors at the base of the leaf stalks. Defoliation prevents transpiration of water from the leaves while they are awaiting planting. If, however, there are signs of their having lost moisture when they arrive, causing shrivelling of the stems to commence, each bush should be completely immersed in water and allowed to remain there for as long as 24 hours if need be. Usually in this time, the stems will plump up and look quite normal.

If the packages of rose trees are received during a period of severe frost, they should be left unopened and the question of defoliation should be left until just before planting because with present-day packaging, particularly when it is composed of polythene, there is little chance of much more deterioration arising from drying out. The wrapped roses should be put into a frost-proof building until the bad weather breaks. During this period of temporary storage, the whole bundle should be, unless it is wrapped in polythene, kept covered with sacking and watered to keep the roses moist. On no account must they be allowed to dry out. Kept under these conditions they will be quite safe for two weeks or more.

It must also be remembered that roses must not be planted in severely wet weather, when the soil is soggy, especially if it is clay. If roses are received when such conditions reign, they should be unpacked, and placed in a trench, which should be in a sheltered part of the garden, and their roots and part of their stems covered with soil. They can safely remain there until the soil becomes good for planting again.

Central and Side-Growing Roots

When the time comes to plant the roses that have been received it will be observed that some of them have their roots rather neatly distributed in all directions around the union, whereas others will have roots that are side-growing (See illustrations on pages 71–72). This will apply equally to bush, standard and climbing roses. As will be appreciated later, when choosing climbers that are intended to be trained up a wall, it is an advantage to choose plants that have

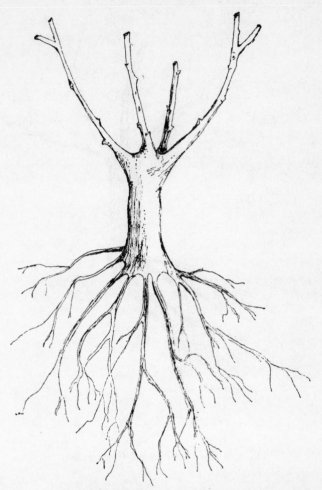

FIG. 4. *A Rose Bush with Central Roots*

side-growing roots (See page 77). In all cases, the actual planting procedure is determined by the manner in which the roots grow from the main stem.

Planting

As a preliminary, for the purpose of giving newly planted varieties a good start in their new quarters, a planting mixture should be

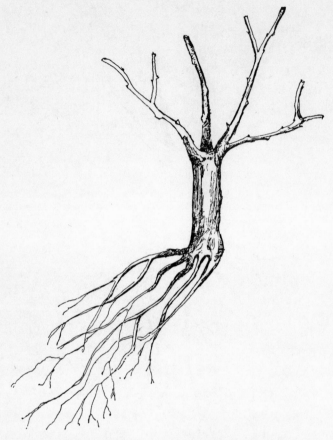

FIG. 5. *A Rose Bush with Side-Growing Roots*

prepared. This is made by taking a large bucket (three gallon size), filling it with moist, granulated peat and adding to it a double handful of raw bonemeal and a handful of hoof and horn meal. All the ingredients are mixed thoroughly together.

Bush Roses

As mentioned previously, the actual process of planting depends upon whether a rose has central – or side-growing roots. In the case of the former, a hole is dug of sufficient diameter that the tree's roots can be spread in it, as near horizontal as possible, usually a hole 12 inches across is satisfactory for this purpose, and of such a depth that the union between the stock and scion will be level with the surface of the earth, when planting is completed.

The soil at the bottom of the hole is mixed thoroughly with two handfuls of the planting mixture, described above, and this soil is then drawn up into a low hummock in the centre of the hole. The crown of the rose is rested on this heap and the roots are spread out as far as possible equally in all directions (See Fig. 6 below). Care should be taken to see that as few as possible of them are crossing. The roots are then covered with a further quantity of the planting mixture, mixed with some of the soil excavated from the hole. The rose should then be subjected to a gentle up and down shaking movement in order to minimise the risk of air pockets being formed.

If the roses are being planted in heavy soil, it is an advantage to add a little sand as this will assist in the formation of good new roots at an early date. Following this, up to about one-third of the excavated soil is added, and then holding the tips of one of the rose's stems, so as to be sure that the union is not lowered, the soil around the rose is gently trodden in, commencing near the circumference of the hole and slowly working inwards towards the central stem. This also lessens the risk of the plant being lowered. The remainder of the soil is then replaced in the hole, left loose and levelled off. It should, however, be noted that if the soil is heavy clay, it should be only

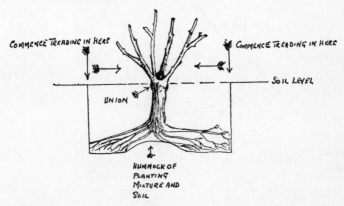

FIG. 6. *Diagram Showing Planting of a Rose with Centrally-Growing Roots*

trodden in very lightly and just sufficiently to consolidate it. If, for
any reason, it becomes imperative to plant roses, when the soil is
very moist, the same rule must be observed. The latter must, however, be a very exceptional happening, because it cannot be over-
emphasised how important it is to plant out roses only when the soil
is just moist and friable.

When dealing with roses with side-growing roots, this procedure
has to be modified. In this case, the planting mixture and soil at the
bottom of the hole, instead of being formed into a central hummock,
is drawn up to one side so that the bottom of the hole is sloping at an
incline with a gradient of approximately the same angle as the roots
are growing in relation to the vertical direction. As before the
roots are carefully spread out and the procedure is from then onwards exactly the same as in the case of roses that have centrally
growing roots, except that treading in should commence above the
extremities of the roots and proceed gradually towards the union, so
that the plant is not lowered in the soil during the operation (See
Fig. 7, below).

Regarding planting distances of bush roses, these are mainly
determined by the vigour of the varieties that are being put in.

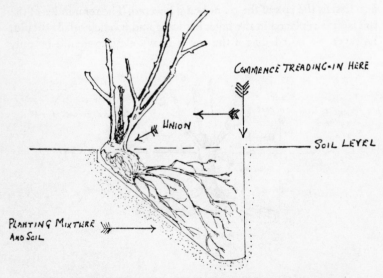

Fig. 7. *Diagram Showing Planting of a Rose with Side-Growing Roots*

Normally it is quite satisfactory to allow 18 to 24 inches between each plant, but in the case of very vigorous roses this has to be extended to 30 inches or more to avoid overcrowding. A final decision on this can best be reached by observing whenever possible the vigour, and width, to which they ultimately grow, of such cultivars that have been chosen, when they are growing under garden conditions, It is also very important to be sure that a space, 12 inches wide, is allowed between the first row in any bed and its edge, otherwise the most disastrous effects on the ladies' stockings are likely, when they stroll along the paths between the beds. In addition, the roses themselves are likely to be damaged when the grass is mown if sufficient space is not allowed.

Standard Roses

Much the same procedure is followed in planting standard roses as with bushes, except in two respects. In the case of this type of rose, the union between the rootstock and the scion is of course at the head of the tall stem. In consequence, this cannot be a criterion of the depth to which they should be planted. Very approximately they should be planted in general to about the same depth as bush roses. If, however they are budded on to rugosa stems, and often standard roses are, they should be planted as shallow as possible, with their upper roots not more than three or four inches below the soil's surface. It is always possible to see when rugosa rootstocks have been used because unlike briar, which has large thorns well spread along the stem, they have a large number of very fine spines, almost touching another, along the whole length of the stem.

The way in which standards differ from bush roses is that they need staking in order to prevent them swaying in the wind and perhaps becoming uprooted. The stake, which should be of such a length that it reaches just below the union, after it is buried some 12 inches in the ground, should be driven in between the roots, so as to avoid them, when the latter are spread out in the hole. Otherwise they are likely to be damaged. When this has been done, the hole is filled and the soil trodden in exactly as in the case of a bush. In addition, planting mixture should be similarly incorporated with the soil at the bottom of the hole.

When the planting of a standard rose is completed, it is necessary to fix it to the stake. To be really satisfactory, it should be tied at three points, viz., just above the ground level, about half-way up the stake and just below the union, near the top (See Fig. 8, below). For this purpose, it is possible to purchase very useful patent ties, which are easy to fix and long lasting. Alternatively, almost

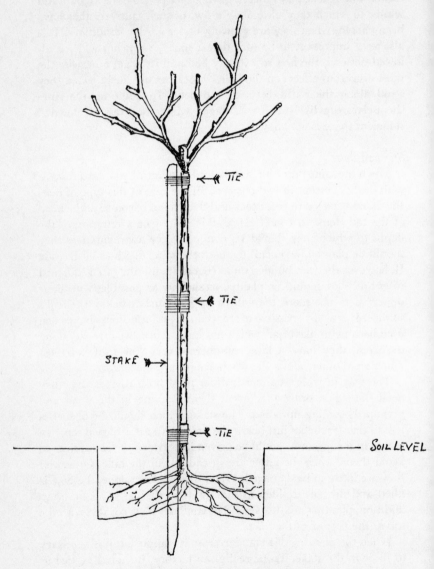

FIG. 8. *Staking a Standard Rose*

without cost, it is quite effective to use tarred twine. In this case, however, it is necessary to wrap several layers of sacking or webbing around the stem at the point of tying in order to prevent any damage being done to the bark. If this is not done, there is a risk of the string cutting into it as the standard grows and creating a weak point. This might lead to the standard being decapitated, when it is exposed to high winds.

Climbing Roses

The procedure for planting climbing roses is exactly the same as it is for bushes. When, however, one is planted against the wall of a house, because the soil is often shallow, due to the presence of foundations, and dry, it should be placed 12 to 15 inches from it and trained back on it. Thus, it can be seen why, as suggested on page 70 it is better to choose a climber with side-growing roots for this purpose. If it is planted so that the root tips are pointing outwards, they should be able to find moisture more easily.

Another point that should also be remembered, particularly when making a garden of a newly built house, is that the soil against the house might have a relatively high lime content, due to the mortar that has been dropped by the bricklayers. It is as well therefore to test the soil with one of the simple acidity testing kits that are available or, alternatively, send a sample of the soil away for analysis. Should it prove to have a pH value above 7.0, then probably the best thing is to replace the soil with some that is more on the acid side. If, however, the bed is a large one, planting should be postponed, until its pH value has been made more suitable for roses by incorporating large quantities of peat in it.

Planting is quite a simple operation, but it is one that should be approached very seriously because in the normal way a gardener plants roses in their permanent quarters, where they are likely to remain for a good many years. It might be for the rest of his life, if they are carefully tended. It pays therefore to carry out this task with diligence because any neglect at this stage might cause them to fail soon and much pleasure would be lost.

CHAPTER EIGHT

Feeding Roses

Although roses do not require heavy feeding, they are very appreciative of relatively small doses of correctly balanced mixtures of fertilizers at regular intervals. They certainly respond well to any such treatment. Later in this chapter, it is the intention to discuss in greater detail the questions of the nutritional requirements of roses, the functions of the various chemicals in the metabolism of plants and the sources from which these elements are derived. In the meantime, however, straightforward recommendations for fertilizing roses are given so that those gardeners who wish to grow good roses can be well equipped with the means of doing so.

The programme for fertilizing roses begins in later winter. Probably February, when usually the worst of the winter weather is over, is the best date. This first action consists of giving a dressing of a slow-acting fertilizer, containing phosphorus and a relatively small amount of nitrogen. It should be of an organic nature, so that it acts as a soil conditioner and breaks down slowly, and thus provides these essential plant foods over a long time. Ideally, two handfuls of meat and bone meal per square yard meet this requirement, but unfortunately in these days this does not seem to be very readily available because of its popularity for animal feeding. Alternatives are bonemeal and fishmeal put down at the same rate.

The next application of fertilizer should be made later on in the spring. This normally consists of a balanced mixture of inorganic chemicals. It is possible of course for the more meticulous gardeners, particularly those who carry out soil analysis, to mix their own, which would naturally match the need that their testing reveals, but in general it is much easier for the average person to buy one of the very excellent compound rose fertilizers that are on the market in these days. A warning should be given, however, to be sure that it is one that has been blended especially for roses, and not a general fertilizer, because sometimes the latter derives its potash content from 'Muriate of Potash' (Potassium chloride), which is a deadly chemical as far as roses are concerned. If a proprietary rose fertilizer mixture is used, it should be put down in accordance with the manufacturer's directions. Another advantage of using commercially compounded fertilizers is that usually they contain trace elements. These are required in such minute quantities that they are difficult for an amateur to incorporate.

For those gardeners who do wish, however, to prepare their own feed, the following can be recommended as a good well-balanced formula.

	lbs
Nitrate of Potash	3
Sulphate of Ammonia	$1\frac{1}{2}$
Superphosphate of Lime	8
Sulphate of Potash	4
Epsom Salts (Magnesium Sulphate)	1
Sulphate of iron	$\frac{1}{4}$
	$17\frac{3}{4}$

In chalky soil, because these elements sometimes get converted into forms that are inaccessible to roses, it is recommended that the weights of the magnesium and iron salts be doubled. Also for the purpose of physically conditioning the soil, when it is heavy clay, it is a good thing to include, in addition, in the above recipe, 3 lb of gypsum, which is calcium sulphate. This chemical, being so insoluble in water, has no chemical effect on the soil.

All these ingredients must of course be thoroughly mixed together. This is best done by putting all of them in a heap on a sheet of polythene of adequate size, spread out on a stone or concrete area and weighted down at its corners with bricks, and turning them over with a spade or trowel, according to the quantity involved, until they are intimately mixed. If there is no need to be over particular, the polythene may be dispensed with, but sometimes stone or concrete becomes stained brown, when it comes in contact with sulphate of iron.

This mixture should be used as a dressing covering the surface of the rose beds at the rate of two ounces (about a handful) per square yard. It should be put down in two doses – the first in mid-May and the second in mid-June, watering it well in afterwards. It is inadvisable to use this mixture later on in the summer, e.g. in late

July or August, because it is likely to produce lush growth, which might not stand the early winter frosts.

The weight of fertilizer provided by this formula is sufficient to give two doses to about 180 roses. This emphasises that, unless a very large number of them are involved, mixing one's own fertilizer is not really worth-while.

How Roses obtain their Food

Unlike animals, plants obtain the very complex compounds, that are needed for their metabolism by synthesising them from very simple chemical compounds. At the outset, it is pointed out that one of the simplest of these is water, which plays a most important role in the very complicated chemical processes that go on in plant tissue. In the modern teaching of chemistry, pupils are nowadays taught to think of water as a chemical, just as much important in its reactions as those of the most abstruse organic chemicals. To appreciate the full significance of providing ample supplies of water for a plant, gardeners might do well to follow the example of the modern schoolboy and think along these lines themselves.

Now all plants manufacture their foodstuffs in the same way and the seat of this activity is situated in their leaves. The raw materials, that they need for this process, are obtained either from the atmosphere or the soil. In order that life can be sustained a plant needs a large array of complex compounds which includes substances like starches, sugars, proteins, enzymes, fats, chlorophyll, all of which have to be synthesised from the simple chemicals that these two sources of supply provide.

The first most important food that is required by all forms of plant life is sugar. This is produced in the leaves by a process that is known as 'photosynthesis'. In this, carbon dioxide is breathed in by the leaves and combined in their cells with water from the soil, to form a simple sugar. This reaction is brought about by the presence of the pigment, chlorophyll, acting as a catalyst and the energy-giving rays of the sun. If the sugar, that is produced by photosynthesis, which is a continuous process operating during the hours of sunlight, is not required immediately, it is turned into starch and is stored in various parts of the plant for future use.

At the same time, other essential chemicals, such as proteins, nucleic acids, phospholipids, fatty acids and many others, are manufactured in the plants. These require, in addition to water, sugars and starches, supplies of the other elements, such as nitrogen, phosphorus (phosphate), potassium (potash), manganese, magnesium, iron, boron, sulphur, copper, molybdenum and zinc. These are all obtained from the soil and are brought to the plant's manufacturing centres in the tissue by way of the roots and stalks, through the agency of the sap. All these, and others, are absolute 'musts' if roses, or any other plants for that matter, are to be maintained healthy and flourishing. If these are not available in the correct balance, their metabolism would eventually break down and the plants would fail to live. Thus if there is any reason to believe that any of them are missing from the soil, it must be provided by the grower. Hence the reason for fertilizing the soil.

The Essential Plant Food Requirements of Roses

In order that a rose grower can have a greater appreciation of the reasons for giving certain elements, in the next few paragraphs, the functions of the more important of them are given together with details of the symptoms, that are shown by roses that are failing to acquire an adequate supply of them, are described. After that, in order to put the subject on to a more practical plane, details are given regarding the sources that provide these essential plant foods so that a gardener can give at any time to his soil anything that it lacks.

The various elements needed for the well-being of roses can be separated into two classes. Firstly, there are the *major nutrient elements*, such as nitrogen, potassium, phosphorus, magnesium, sulphur and calcium which are needed in large amounts and, secondly, the *minor nutrient elements*, *micro-elements* or *trace elements*, of which plants only need the minutest amounts, and which in fact are detrimental if fed in large doses. Among these are iron, manganese, copper, boron, molybdenum and zinc.

The Major Nutrient Elements

Nitrogen. This element is a constituent of all proteins, enzymes and the most important of all plant pigments, chlorophyll. Although the life of a rose cannot be sustained without it, excessive quantities can lead to soft and lush growth, which is often weak and a ready victim to disease and to frost damage in the winter. For this reason, nitrogen in the form of an artificial fertilizer should never be given late in the growing season. In addition, an excess gives poor quality flowers because the bushes are forced to make a profusion of foliage at their expense.

Nitrogen deficiency is characterised by a gradual fading of the green colour of the leaves which ultimately turn yellow. Sometimes this change of colour is accompanied by the reddening of the leaves in the vicinity of the veins. This is due to the excessive production of certain red colouring matters, found in plants – the anthrocyanin pigments. In addition, if this condition is allowed to continue, the growth in spring is feeble. The more soluble forms of nitrogen – nitrates and ammonium compounds – are given as a tonic when they are needed, such as after the winter rains have depleted the soil of its readily accessible supplies of nitrogen.

Phosphorus (Phosphate). Phosphorus deficiency and that of nitrogen are the two most commonly encountered in agriculture and horti-culture. One difficulty is that the former element has a tendency to combine with other compounds to form chemical complexes that are insoluble, and so become unavailable as a plant food. Another danger is that the symptoms of phosphorus deficiency are not so spectacular as those of nitrogen and so are less readily detected. This element plays a very important role in the metabolism of a plant and is a constituent of a number of vitally important substances, such as proteins and phospholipids. Another very significant point of this element is its close association with nucleic acids and their relation with tissue cells. Thus lack of phosphorus, in consequence of the latter, has a serious effect on the growth of the plant by limiting cell division. The main part played however, by phosphorus is in relation to the energy transfers, which are involved, especially in leaf respiration and in photosynthesis, by which process a plant derives its starch foods.

It helps to promote the well-being of plants, gives rise to earlier growth, hastens the ripening of wood and hardens plants, so that they resist bad winter conditions and die back, and encourages the formation of better root systems. Without it, growth is always stunted and the leaves, while remaining intensely green, may have tinges of red on them.

Potassium (Potash). This element is not a direct component of any important plant chemicals, but it nevertheless plays a very important role in the carbohydrate metabolism and its absence has a very serious effect on plants. When there is a deficiency, the stems become mechanically weak and bend or snap off easily and there is a degeneration of what are known by botanists as sieve tubes, which are concerned with the transport of food material about the plant. Roses lacking this element have a greater susceptibility to disease and frost damage than those that are well supplied with it. The signs of its absence are that the leaves become yellow at their tips and round their margins, and such organs as roots tubers and seeds, where foods are normally stored, are poorly developed. Potassium deficiency is more common in light sandy and chalky soil than in heavier ones. This element is so important that it is essential to be sure that any compound manure used for roses has a high potassium content.

Calcium. Usually there are ample supplies of this element in the soil. It is largely concerned in plants with maintaining the efficient working of the tissue cells, and is also a constituent of calcium pectate, which is a cementing agent that binds the cells together. If there is a deficiency of this element, there is a rapid breakdown of the apical growing points of the stems and roots. An early sign of a shortage is malformation of the young leaves as they appear. Calcium is of course concerned with the regulation of the acidity of the soil. Calcium deficiency does not normally occur very frequently in plants. Usually long before its symptoms appear, plants show signs of suffering from high soil acidity.

Magnesium. The great importance of this element in the vegetable kingdom is that it is an essential component of chlorophyll and is necessary for the production of this vital pigment. Its deficiency is more usually signalled by the yellowing first of the older leaves and ultimately the younger ones.

Minor Nutrient Elements

Iron. This element, while it is not a constituent of the vital pigment, chlorophyll, is essential to its production. If a deficiency arises, the effects are dramatised by their very sudden appearance and the yellowing of the younger leaves, still leaving their veins green. It is characterised by those leaves, that were produced before the onset of the attack, remaining unaffected (See Chlorosis, page 149).

Manganese. Deficiency of manganese is very difficult to distinguish from that caused by the lack of magnesium. Like iron, it is not a component of chlorophyll, but is very closely concerned with its manufacture in the plant.

Regarding the remaining trace elements, viz., copper, boron, molybdenum and zinc, that have already been mentioned, although it is known that their absence in the soil can lead to deleterious effects, their full significance is not entirely understood. They have, however, an importance in plant metabolism in relation to enzymes, which are substances that catalyse various vital processes. Some of them are known to be pure proteins and act on their own, but others have to be chemically coupled with certain non-protein compounds, which are known as *co-enzymes* or *prosthetic agents*. If this combination does not exist, these specific enzymes are inert. The minor nutrient elements, boron, copper, molybdenum and zinc, are all known to be associated with these co-enzymes.

Sources of the Most Important Plant Foods

Fertilizers may either be organic or inorganic (artificial). There is a simple difference between these two types. The former are either produced directly from animal or vegetable sources as is the case with farmyard manure, garden compost, or are materials from such sources, that are processed, such as bonemeal, meat and bone meal. The latter are artificially produced chemicals. Examples of these are sulphate of ammonia and potassium nitrate. The other very important distinction is that the naturally produced fertilizers are composed of complex chemical compounds, which have to be broken down by the action of the soil bacteria into simpler substances that can be absorbed by the plants. They are therefore slow-acting. On the other hand, the artificials are simple soluble salts and are thus quick-acting. Organic fertilizers are therefore put down on the ground long before they are likely to be needed, whereas the fast-acting chemical fertilizers can be distributed more immediately in order to obtain early results and to produce a tonic effect. For example, after a long dry spell, during which copious watering has been carried out, the soluble nitrogen content of the soil may have been leached out. A small dose of sulphate of ammonia would very rapidly rectify this defect.

A well-planned fertilizing programme should contain both slow-acting fertilizers, that supply the essential elements steadily over a long period so that a certain amount of them is always present in the soil and fast-acting ones, which are designed to provide for the plant's various needs as they arise during the growing season. The fertilizing programme for roses described in the opening paragraphs of this chapter is typical.

There is one great advantage in using organic fertilizers, such as farmyard manure, sewage compost, garden compost, spent hops, that should be borne in mind. This is that they have a high humus content, which helps to improve the moisture retention powers of the soil. Although it is rather expensive to use on a large scale, peat is also an excellent source of humus, but it must be remembered that it has no nutrient value. If it is used therefore it must be supplemented with a balanced mixture of plant foods.

In the following tables, the main sources of the three major nutrient elements needed by roses are given with the approximate percentage of each element that they contain.

NITROGEN

Material	Nitrogen Content (%)	Other Details
ARTIFICIAL		
Ammonium Nitrate	35	Very soluble so acts quickly
Ammonium Sulphate	21	Soluble. Acts quickly.
Sodium Nitrate	16	Acts immediately.
Potassium Nitrate	14	Acts quickly.
ORGANIC		
Dried Blood	9–14	Moderately fast-acting.
Hoof and Horn Meal	8–14	Totally assimulated by plants in six weeks. Releases nitrogen fairly quickly.
Bonemeal	3–4	Also contains 20–25% Phosphate.
Meat and Bone Meal	5	Also contains 16–20% Phosphate.
Fishmeal	6–10	Also contains 6–14% Phosphate.
Soot	3–6	Also contains 6–14% Phosphate.

PHOSPHORUS (PHOSPHATE)

Material	*Phosphate Content (%)*	*Other Details*
ARTIFICIAL		
Superphosphate (Superphosphate of lime)	20	This is both a short and long term source of phosphate. Part of it is rapid in action, while the rest is converted into a less soluble form when mixed with soil. This portion remains available to the plant for an appreciable time. When put down with sulphate of ammonia, its efficiency is increased.
Ammonium Phosphate	48	Also contains 11% nitrogen. Readily soluble and quick-acting.
ORGANIC		
Bonemeal	21	Also contains 3–5% nitrogen. Is slow-acting.
Steamed bonemeal	28	Faster acting than bonemeal.

POTASH (POTASSIUM)

Material	*Potash Content (%)*	*Other Details*
ARTIFICIAL		
Potassium Nitrate	46	Acts quickly. Also contains 13% nitrogen.
Potassium Sulphate	48	Is quick acting. It is soluble in water, but it is not so easily washed out of the soil as other chemical salts. It does not burn the roots and is therefore suitable to use in composts intended for roses grown in pots.
ORGANIC		
Wood Ash	4 to 10	Acts immediately. Must be kept dry while being stored.

Organic Fertilizers Supplying Nitrogen, Phosphorus and Potassium

There are several organic fertilizers that are sources, to a greater or lesser degree, of the three major nutrient elements, Nitrogen, Phosphorus and Potassium. They are also, of course, excellent sources of humus. The analysis of these are given below:—

	Nitrogen %	Phosphate %	Potash %
Farmyard Manure	2.0	0.9	2.0
Poultry Manure, raw	4.0	3.5	1.75
Poultry Manure, deep litter	3.0	4.0	2.0
Garden Compost	2.0	0.5	0.75
Spent Hops	3.0	1.5	trace
Sewage Sludge	4.5	3.0	0.5

Foliar Feeding

It has been known for a long time that the leaves of roses are able to absorb simple chemical plant foods. Thus plants can be fertilized by spraying them with solutions containing essential nutrients. This process is known as foliar feeding. This is not, however, a substitute for a fertilization programme, such as that already discussed, but it is a means of dealing with any emergency that might arise. There are various circumstances under which roses might benefit from this first aid treatment. For instance, during a dry, cold spring, the sap may not have risen sufficiently to bring the essential plant foods from the soil to the leaves, where they are to be converted; it could be that drought during the summer has necessitated heavy watering, or it might have been an exceptionally wet season, both of which might have leached the important nutrients out of the soil at a time when the roses most need them. Again, in chalky soil, sometimes iron and magnesium are trapped in chemical substances, that are unassimilable by the plants, and supplies of these elements are urgently needed if they are to survive. All these are typical situations that can be adequately met by foliar feeding.

This task is best carried out early in the morning or in the evening, but never in bright sun, because of the risk of scorching the leaves. As with solid fertilizers, it is usually better for the amateur to purchase a proprietary foliar feed, especially blended for roses. Anybody, however, who wishes to make his own, should mix together one part by weight of potassium acid phosphate and two parts by weight of urea, both of which can be bought at a chemist. An ounce of this mixture should be dissolved in a gallon of water. These two chemicals when dissolved in water, are not stable, so a fresh solution should be made up on each occasion.

CHAPTER NINE

Pruning Roses

Why Prune Roses?

In order to understand the reason why it is the practice to prune roses regularly, it is important for a gardener to appreciate the difference that exists between roses and other trees and shrubs. In many cases, the latter keep growing in all directions until they reach maturity, when they cease to become any larger. Thus, unless they are growing in gardens, where sometimes it is necessary to restrict their size, they are never cut back at all. Often, if they are, they lose a considerable amount of their beauty.

Roses, however, are different. If it were possible to watch the habit of a wild dog rose growing in a hedgerow over several years, it would be seen that it throws up initially two or three strong shoots from its base. These will grow vigorously, producing healthy foliage and flowers very freely. As the years pass by, there will be a noticeable reduction in their vigour and ultimately further young shoots will spring into life from the ground level and their robustness will steal nourishment from the old shoots. Slowly the older growth will be starved and disease will attack it and it will finally give up and die. While they are gradually passing away these old shoots in their struggle for survival will be taking water and nourishment that could be better utilized by the new healthy ones that have a brighter future. What will have been observed is in fact nature's own way of pruning roses and of ensuring that a good healthy vigorous plant survives. It will be appreciated that this is a rather slow and wasteful process, which gardeners have found to be unsatisfactory because it gives an unsightly appearance in their gardens and fosters the spread of diseases from the dying shoots, which make excellent hosts for them. Thus, pruning, as we know it, has been introduced as a means of eliminating the disadvantages of letting nature follow her own course.

When one appreciates the manner in which this task is undertaken in the wild, it must be realized that pruning is a very simple operation that can be carried out very easily by any intelligent gardener. In fact, the famous German rose breeder, Wilhelm

Kordes, in his book *Roses* says 'Always remember that the real art of pruning lies in removing all useless wood, i.e. wood that has become weak and exhausted with age or from the effect of frost. Weak, unripe shoots, which will probably never develop into strong branches, may also be removed. Otherwise let the plant live.'

Perhaps before discussing this operation in greater detail, it is as well to enumerate the chief objects of pruning. They are:

(1) To encourage growth.
(2) To maintain good health by removing diseased wood and dead wood that is likely to become affected by disease.
(3) To minimise the risk of the spread of infection.
(4) To shape the plant and fit it into its position in the garden.
(5) To keep the plant young by continuously cutting out old wood and encouraging the growth of young stems from its base.
(6) To restrict the number of flower shoots, when large exhibition blooms are required.

Despite these very straightforward aims and the simplicity of the process, as mentioned in Chapter 1, there has been considerable controversy in gardening circles during recent years on how and when pruning of roses should be carried out. So much so that the task has been made to appear a rather frightening one, and many beginners have become confused. In the next few paragraphs, it is hoped to eliminate a good deal of the worry that some rose-growers might have on this comparatively simple subject.

Methods of Pruning

So that the explanations, that will be given below, can be fully understood, it is necessary to provide some general preliminary details. In the first place if a rose stem of any type is examined, it will be observed that all along it there are a series of 'buds' or 'eyes', which alternatively point more or less inwards and outwards. When pruning, with one exception that will be discussed later, the cut is made just above an outward growing bud. Secondly, gardeners speak of three types of pruning, viz., 'hard', 'moderate' and 'light'. Dealing with the last-mentioned first, this more or less means just removing the dead flowers or hips by cutting the stem at the first or second eye below the flower-bearing foot-stalk. (See Fig. 13 on page 99). This is mainly carried out when pruning floribunda

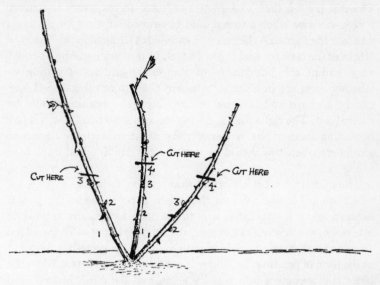

FIG. 9. *Pruning*

In the Spring following planting, new hybrid tea and floribunda roses
are *hard pruned*, i.e. cut back to the third or fourth bud from ground,
whichever is growing outwards

and shrub roses. Hard pruning (see Fig. 9), which is largely restricted to the first spring after the roses have been planted out in
the garden, consists of cutting each stem back to three or four buds,
whichever is pointing outwards, from the ground, so that the bushes
are probably no more than six to eight inches high. Lastly 'moderate'
pruning, which is the most frequently practised method, consists of
cutting back the main stems and strong laterals to an outwards-
growing bud about halfway along their length (See Fig 12 on page
97).

When Should Roses be Pruned?

There is no doubt that many beginners have become very
confused in recent years because they have been told, perhaps by old
stagers, that roses must be pruned at *no* other time than during the
last two weeks of March, while other more advanced thinkers are
met afterwards who advocate varying times in the year, from October onwards as being the most suitable. How very confusing it all is!

The real truth is that, to a greater or lesser degree, every contender is right because when a rose should be pruned largely depends upon whether the garden is sheltered or exposed or situated in the South or North of the country and so on. In fact, in the very extreme, it could vary within the boundaries of the same garden, according to whether roses are in a sheltered warm position or otherwise. There can be no hard and fast rule on the date when pruning should be carried out. The right time is during the winter, when the sap is just beginning to rise. Nature herself very accommodatingly signals to gardeners when this should be done by the swelling and reddening of the eyes.

The reason why it is important that pruning should be carried out when the sap is just rising is that when a cut is made, the pith is exposed and it is imperative that this is healed as rapidly as possible otherwise, if a severe frost comes, the shoot is likely to be damaged and fungus diseases are able to get a hold. If the growth is dormant at the time of pruning, healing will not take place, whereas when the plant is just coming into activity again and the sap is just rising it will heal without delay. On the other hand, if the sap is flowing freely, as it might be in early autumn or late spring, the shoot is likely to bleed after being cut. Thus, it will be seen that the time for pruning depends entirely upon whether the cut can heal before it is likely to be damaged by frost.

It is obvious therefore that in milder and more sheltered parts, pruning might be done at almost any time in the winter because the growth is seldom dormant. It could in some cases be in October, but it always seems such a great shame to cut down the roses so early and lose all the beautiful colour that they give so generously during the autumn. In many parts, February is a good month to prune because by that time the severest weather of the winter has passed and plant life is beginning to stir. In Northern and very cold exposed areas, it is of course often necessary to wait until the end of March, or even early April in some years. Thus it will be seen that the right time to prune roses is something that strictly individual gardeners must work out for themselves, according to the climatic conditions under which they live and the indications that the roses in their gardens give them.

How to Prune Roses

For a long time it was always advocated that roses should always be hard pruned – and there are still some adherents to this rule living today. It was always maintained that the weaker the growth the greater the extent to which the plant should be sheared down. During the last twenty years or so, there has gradually arisen a rival faction that advocates that present-day roses should be moderately pruned, i.e. their main stems and strong-growing laterals should be cut back to about halfway, otherwise they will not flower well. Taking into account the facts that are known about our modern roses, it is highly probable that they are right because most of them are rather different in their origin, their vigour and habits than they were twenty-five years ago.

At about this time, the very wonderful hybrid rose, Peace, was introduced. This had characteristics that had rarely, perhaps never, been seen in a hybrid tea before. It had excessive vigour, it grew tall, and it produced outsize blooms. It was, however, soon found by some of the hard-bitten older gardeners that, when it was given the hard-pruning treatment, which was their life-long practice, it showed its resentment by producing a lot of leaves and blind shoots and by becoming shy of blooming. Now, being such an exceptional rose, Peace is the forebear of a large proportion of our modern garden roses and it has not only passed on to them its great vigour and tall-growing habit, but also its resentment of being cut back too hard. If the pedigree of Peace is examined a little more closely it will be found that among its forebears is a species rose, *Rosa foetida bicolor*, which is a sport of the very ancient *Rosa foetida* (*R. lutea*), which is also known to dislike being cut back severely. This appears to justify the current practice of pruning our present-day roses moderately, rather than to cut them almost to the ground each spring, as was the practice with the older types of hybrid tea roses, many of which have now disappeared from the nurserymen's catalogues. The actual procedure for pruning various types of roses is described in detail later.

Tools Required for Pruning

In these days, secateurs are almost entirely used for pruning roses. This is rather a pity because by far the most satisfactory way is to do it with a pruning knife because a cleaner cut can be made. The biggest danger with secateurs is that there is always a great risk of the stalks being crushed. Although it is difficult to use a knife skilfully at first, it is well worth a gardener devoting a little time to mastering this art. The first essential is for the knife to be razor sharp, and to this end it should be continuously sharpened on a carborundum stone during pruning. To prune with a knife, the operator should hold the shoot at its tip with the left hand, bending it slightly towards him and cut it at the selected place by drawing the knife across it, commencing at the base of the blade. Secateurs can be used for cutting out the dead wood and the very old tough branches can be removed with a pruning saw. When pruning, practising good hygiene is an essential. A 10% solution of trisodium acid orthophosphate should always be at hand so that the blade of the knife or secateurs can be dipped into it after a diseased shoot has been eliminated.

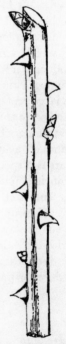

FIG. 10. *Correct Pruning*

The shoot is pruned with an upward-sloping cut, commencing with its lower point at the level of the base of the bud on the side opposite it and ending with its higher point about ¼ inch above the base of the eye on the other

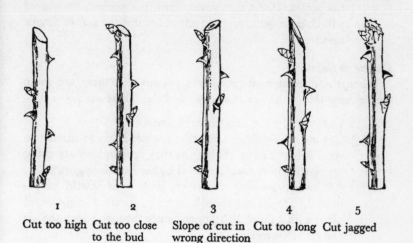

1	2	3	4	5
Cut too high	Cut too close to the bud	Slope of cut in wrong direction	Cut too long	Cut jagged

FIG. 11. *Faulty Pruning*

How to make the Cut

In pruning there is a certain technique that must be followed in making the cut. The first rule is that, with one exception (see page 96), a rose is always pruned at an outward-growing bud. The other is that the cut is made sloping, commencing with the lower point at the level of the base of the bud on the side opposite to it and ending with its higher point about $\frac{1}{4}$ inch above the base of the eye, on the other side. Correct pruning is illustrated in Fig. 10 on page 94.

There are a number of ways in which a cut must not be made when pruning. These are illustrated in Fig. 11. They are:—

(1) *Cut too high.* If the shoot is cut high above the bud, it will die back to it and it might become a seat of infection.

(2) *Cut too close to the bud.* In this case, the bud is likely to be damaged. A malformed shoot would develop.

(3) *Cut with slope in the wrong direction.* The principal reason for making a sloping cut in the manner described is to allow the rain to run off away from the bud. If the slope is in the wrong direction this will not happen.

(4) *Cut too long.* If this is done, an unduly large amount of pith is exposed and healing is prolonged, during which period damage might be done to the shoot.

(5) *Cut jagged.* If the cut is not clean, but jagged, the tissues will be damaged and they might become the seat of fungus infection.

Pruning in General

When the operation of pruning is commenced there are three preliminary things that must always be done. These are:—

(1) Cut out all dead and diseased wood.
(2) Cut out all weak growths that are not likely to mature to good robust shoots. As long as they remain they are using up nourishment that is needed by the healthier growths.
(3) All inward-growing shoots on bush roses should be removed. The object should be to maintain a cup-shaped plant with a good, light, open centre through which the air can circulate freely.

In the case of a bush that has a prostrate growing habit, in order to achieve this cup-shape, it is sometimes expedient to make an exception to the rule of pruning always at an outward-growing bud, by cutting at an inward – and upward – growing one, so that the new shoots develop upwards and the rose no longer sprawls along the ground.

Pruning Hybrid Tea Roses
First Year Plants

With roses of this age, both the old and new schools of thought on pruning are agreed. In every case, each shoot should be cut back to an outward-growing eye about six to eight inches above the ground; this generally means to three or four buds (Fig. 9, page 91). This is done in order to get as many shoots as possible to grow from low down on the bush so as to obtain a compact, well-balanced tree. It is an interesting thing, but whatever the length a rose shoot is when it is cut back, never more than the three top eyes burst into growth at one time. So if any shoots are left long, an unsightly leggy tree with top-knots of growth will result. By cutting back to three or four eyes from the ground, a good well-proportioned bush will develop quickly.

After The First Year

After all the dead, diseased, weak and inward-growing shoots have been cut out, all the stems, except two of them emerging from the

A formal rose garden at Chateau de Bagatelle, Paris

Alec's Red (Hybrid Tea)
Bright Crimson.
Raised by Cocker, 1970

Mullard Jubilee (Hybrid Tea),
Cerise Pink.
Raised by McGredy, 1970

Silver Star (Hybrid Tea)
Lavender.
Raised by Kordes, 1966

Elizabeth Harkness (Hybrid Tea)
Buff, tinged pink.
Raised by Harkness, 1969

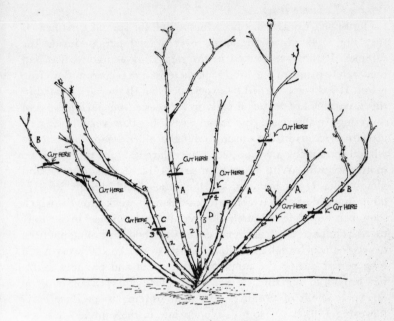

FIG. 12. *Pruning Hybrid Tea Roses After the First Year*

All the dead, diseased, weak and inward-growing shoots are first cut out.
All basal shoots (A), except two (C and D) and all ripe laterals (B) are
pruned moderately, i.e. cut back about half their length at an outward-
growing bud. The two basal shoots (C and D) are hard pruned (to 3
or 4 buds)

base of the rose tree, and the ripe laterals from the old wood are
pruned moderately, i.e. they are cut back to half the length of the
previous year's growth at an outward-growing eye. The remaining
two basal shoots should be hard pruned to about three buds from
the ground. This two-way treatment has been especially developed
for modern vigorous tall-growing hybrid tea roses as a means of
curbing their growth. This procedure is repeated each year. Each
time, different shoots, growing from the base, are selected for
cutting back. By making this choice judiciously, it is possible to
control the size and shape of the bushes without any reduction in
the flowering ability, which might occur, if they were hard pruned
each year (See Fig. 12, above).

D

Pruning Floribunda Roses

Floribunda roses, it has been found, call for special treatment if they are to flower continuously over a long period during the summer. If they are treated in the same way as hybrid teas and moderately pruned their lovely characteristic of recurrent flowering is lost. It has been learned by experience that, if they are treated in this way, they are colourful early in the season, but their period of flowering is shortened by some weeks because very little new growth develops in the autumn and the older wood tends to die without producing any new wood to replace it. Hard pruning is no more successful. With this treatment the plants fail to grow and almost die. Light pruning, on the other hand, results in very large unwieldy trees, which are massed with weak growth, which soon becomes infested with disease. In consequence of a study carried out in recent years, a satisfactory method of pruning has been developed which enables floribunda roses to give good flowers over a long period during the summer and autumn and provides ample new growth to start the new season. This technique is a combination of two methods of pruning, viz., light pruning to produce early flowering and harder to give blooms late in the summer and new growth for the following year.

As with hybrid tea roses, the elimination of all dead, weak, diseased wood and all shoots that are growing across the centre of the bush, so that it is clear and open, are the first essentials. The various steps that follow this preliminary work are outlined below:—

First Year After Planting

As with hybrid tea roses, floribunda roses are hard pruned to three or four eyes above the ground, which usually means that after pruning they are 6 to 9 inches high.

Second Year

All the main shoots that are growing from the base of the bush or from very near to it are all lightly pruned. This is all the new one year old wood. This procedure amounts to just removing the spent flower heads at an outward-growing bud, which should be the second or third one below the pedicel. Any secondary shoots that may have grown from a point just below the base of the flower

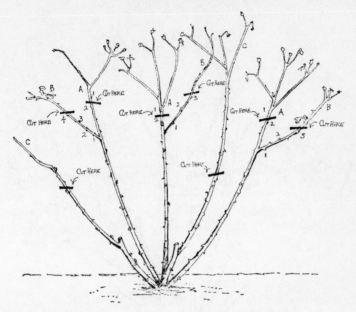

FIG. 13. *Pruning Floribunda Roses in the Second Year*

All the dead, diseased, weak and inward-growing shoots are first cut out. All spent flowers are cut from the one-year-old growth (A), that grows from the base of the bush, at the second or third bud, whichever is growing outwards, below the pedicel, i.e. lightly pruned, any laterals (B), growing just below the pedicel are reduced to three or four eyes in length. All shoots growing from old wood (C), i.e. that pruned last year, is cut back about halfway

clusters should be reduced to a length of three or four eyes, according to which is growing outwards. All the stems that are growing from the remaining old wood, which, in the first year, would have been cut back to three or four eyes, are reduced to about half their length (See Fig. 13, above).

Third and Subsequent Years

In this technique of pruning floribunda roses, unlike with hybrid tea roses, the treatment in the third and subsequent years is different to that in the second. It consists of pruning all the new one-year-old wood, that emanates from low down on the bush, lightly and all the

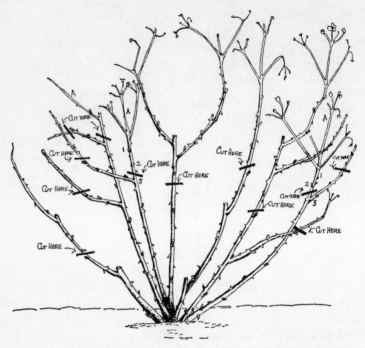

FIG. 14. *Pruning Floribunda Roses in the Third and Subsequent Years*

All the dead, diseased, weak and inward-growing shoots are first cut out. All spent flowers are cut from the one-year-old wood (A), that emanates from low down on the bush, at the second or third bud, whichever is growing outwards, below the pedicel, i.e. lightly pruned. All remaining shoots are moderately pruned, i.e. cut back about halfway at an outward growing eye

remaining old wood moderately. In the next year, the wood, that has been lightly pruned in the third year, will be moderately pruned. In subsequent years a similar procedure will be followed (Fig. 14).

It will be seen that by this method any floribunda rose bush will contain a certain amount of lightly pruned younger growth, which will flower early in the season, and some harder pruned older wood that will throw strong shoots that will commence flowering later in the summer and continue until autumn, possibly to Christmas Day, if the frosts do not come before. Thus a long flowering season can be assured by this more recently developed technique for pruning floribunda roses.

Pruning Standard Rose Trees and Weeping Standards

It will be appreciated that standard hybrid tea and floribundas are the same as the corresponding bush varieties, except that they are budded on to tall stems of rugosa or briar. In principle, therefore, they are treated in the same way as their dwarf counterparts. Keeping a cup-shaped head with a good light open centre is an essential quality that should be aimed at. In most cases it will be found, however, if mostly moderate pruning is carried out the best results are secured.

Weeping Standards

Weeping standards, which are still encountered in some gardens are usually rambler roses that have been budded on tall stems of briar or rugosa. The most satisfactory ramblers for this purpose are those that belong to Group 1 Ramblers (see page 103), which, when grown as climbers, send up their new shoots from the ground. As these are the flowering canes for the next year, these are kept and tied in, whilst those that have already flowered are cut out in autumn. The same principle is applied to a weeping standard, that is a Group 1 Rambler, budded on to briar or rugosa. In this case, the new stems, that will provide next year's flowers, grow from its crown. These are retained and all the older wood is cut out annually. Sometimes Group 2 Ramblers are used for this purpose, but they are not so suitable. These are pruned by removing the old wood, when necessary, and reducing the length of the laterals.

Pruning Rose Species and Shrub Roses

The species and their hybrids need very little pruning other than removing any dead or diseased wood, and anything that is necessary to keep them in a good shape and to regulate their size in relation to the space allowed to them. Shrub roses need rather similar treatment. In the case of those that are remontant it is a particular advantage to remove the dead clusters of flowers by cutting back to the second eye below them. This will encourage further blooming later in the season.

Both species and shrubs eventually, with advancing years, become rather top heavy and bare at their bases. This can be rectified by cutting back several of the main shoots fairly hard in order to induce shoots to break from the lower parts of the plant.

Pruning Miniature Roses

Little or no pruning is required with miniature roses. It is only necessary to remove any spent flowers and dead or diseased wood. If, for any reason, it is required to trim back miniature roses, just as with any other type of roses the cut must be made just above a healthy outward growing eye. The best instrument to use for pruning them is a very sharp pair of nail scissors.

Pruning Polyantha Pompons

These rather charming roses have gone out of fashion in these days, but because of their possible usefulness in modern small gardens, the method of pruning them is given. It is only necessary to cut out the old flower stems to an eye high up on the stalk and to remove any old wood that has ceased to shoot.

Pruning Ramblers and Climbing Roses

It will be recalled that on page 38, it was stated that so complex had become the question of ramblers and climbing roses that rose experts had in recent years resorted to classifying them in accordance with their pruning requirements.

Ramblers were very popular in the more expansive gardens forty years ago, when gardening labour was cheap and easy to obtain. Indeed they always put up a very lovely show! Unfortunately many of the favourites of those days have largely disappeared because of their lack of remontancy, which is an essential in plants for modern small gardens, and the considerable amount of work entailed in pruning them and training them. Despite this, however, there are some more recently introduced varieties that flower recurrently and are far less vigorous. These modern versions of ramblers are grown today and the class has not by any means become extinct.

The modern method of classifying ramblers and climbers is to place them in four classes. The first two of which, Group 1 and Group 2, cover the two types of ramblers, which are mainly hybrids of *Rosa wichuraiana* and *Rosa multiflora* and the remaining categories Group 3 and Group 4 include all the climbing roses, that are not ramblers. The broad distinction between the first two groups and the second two groups is that the members of the former are pruned soon after flowering and in any case not later than early autumn, whereas those of the latter are treated during the winter. In the following paragraphs each group is dealt with in greater detail.

Group 1. Ramblers

The characteristic of the members of this group is that they always grow their new shoots from their bases. Their pruning is comparatively simple, providing it is done as soon after the flowers fade as is possible. Ramblers of this type always bloom on the new wood that was produced in the previous year. Those shoots that have flowered during the current season, if left unattended on the plant, will wane and eventually die. So what has to be done is to remove this old wood as soon after flowering has ceased as possible; and then, and this is very important, to tie in all the new green shoots so that they take up the shape of the object on which the rose is climbing. It is as well to be warned that if pruning and tying in is neglected, the

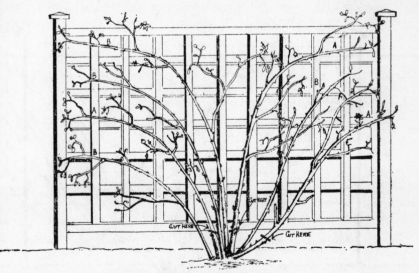

FIG. 15. *Pruning Group I Ramblers*

Ramblers always bloom on the new wood produced in the previous year. All old wood shoots (A), that have flowered during current season, are cut back at an outward-growing bud near the base of the tree. The new shoots (B) are then tied in

rambler will soon become a tangled mass which will be almost impossible to unravel. Crimson Shower, which blooms from late July to mid-September, very rampant-growing rose-pink Dorothy Perkins, bright rose-crimson Excelsa, deep fawn pink François Juranville, deep pink Minnehaha, which is very vigorous and Sanders' White Rambler are all members of this category. (Fig. 15).

Sometimes, when the summer has been very dry, insufficient new growth appears from the base of a rambler. In this case, in order to secure flowering in the next year, some of the previous year's growth should be retained and the laterals cut back to two or three eyes.

Group 2. Ramblers

The roses in this category are characterised by throwing a lesser number, if any, of their new shoots from their bases. They more usually spring from the old wood higher up. This type of rambler is pruned by cutting the old wood back to the point, where a strong new green shoot is emerging. This leading shoot is left and tied in,

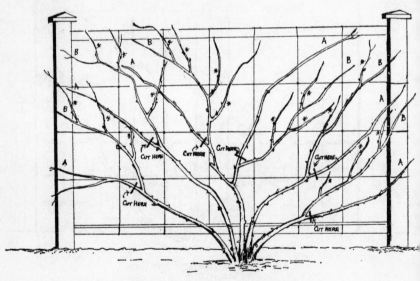

FIG. 16. *Pruning Group II Ramblers*

All old wood leading shoots (A) are pruned back to where a healthy new leading shoot (B) emerges. All laterals on the main shoots retained are cut back to a length of two or three buds at points marked (*)

but any shorter laterals are pruned back to a length of two or three eyes from their point of origin. If there is no new leading shoot on any old wood stem, it should be removed. (Fig. 16.)

Because of their propensity to shoot higher up the stem, Group 2 ramblers often become bare at their lower parts. This can often be remedied by cutting back one or two of the stouter stems to a good dormant eye about 12 to 18 inches from its base.

Ramblers included in this category are Blaze, Dr W. Van Fleet, Easlea's Golden Rambler, the rather less vigorous New Dawn, Veilchenblau and Violette. Both the two last named roses are 'blue' in colour.

Group 3 and 4 Climbers

These two groups contain between them almost everything else among roses that climbs.

Group 3 Climbers

The members of this group are the more vigorous climbers that are more usually used for covering walls, pergolas, fences and some are suitable for hedges. The class includes the stronger growing climbing sports of the hybrid tea and floribunda roses and the more rampant of the Large Flowering Climbers. None of these types of roses should be pruned during the first year of planting as this sometimes gives them such a shock that they revert to the dwarf form. In subsequent years, they should be pruned at any time in late autumn or winter, but not late in the spring after the new growth has started. On no account should any new growth be cut back unless it is damaged or it is occupying too much space. Old exhausted wood should be cut out. The laterals that have flowered should be cut back to about three eyes from the point from which they emanate from the main stem. Sometimes in a dry spring climbing roses are slow to break into new growth. This can be facilitated by spraying the plants with water.

Group 4 Climbers

This group contains the more moderate growing climbing hybrid tea roses and other climbing roses and the pillar roses. Among the latter are the recurrent flowering *kordesii* climbers. They are rather less vigorous than the climbing roses in Group 3 and, with a few exceptions, mostly do not grow more than 10 feet in height, sometimes appreciably less. Apart from cutting out dead, exhausted and diseased wood, they do not require any pruning other than that which is necessary to keep them in good shape and within the compass of the space allocated to them in the garden. Newly planted roses in this group should not be pruned in their first year.

This group includes many of the climbing roses that are suitable for present-day gardens, such as Allen Chandler, Copenhagen, Dortmund, Elegance, Golden Glow, Golden Showers, Climbing Goldilocks, High Noon, Kathleen Harrop, Maigold, Parade, Royal Gold, Soldier Boy and Zéphirine Drouhin. Most of these are modest in their growth, need very little attention and mostly recurrent in flowering.

CHAPTER TEN

The Maintenance of Roses

THE MAINTENANCE OF ROSES
Already two of the very important items in a rose maintenance programme, viz., feeding and pruning, have been dealt with in detail. There are, however, quite a number of other things that have to be done if roses are to flourish. Fortunately, the majority of them are quite simple, but they are nevertheless quite important to the well-being of the plants. It is well worth the time of any gardener who wants the best results to give attention to them. These various tasks are spread throughout the whole of the year, with not unnaturally, a preponderance during the spring and summer. As it is when the former comes that gardeners stir themselves from their indoor winter activities, this is chosen as the starting point of this calendar of work, which is described below.

SPRING

Check up on Stakes, Posts and Ties
Probably one of the earliest essential tasks that has to be done, and this is one that can usually be carried out on a dry day, when it is too soft under foot to do any cultivation in the garden, is to check, and, if necessary, renew the stakes and ties supporting standard and weeping roses and the posts carrying the climbing roses. It could easily be that the winter weather has caused damage, which, if not righted, will lead to injury to the roses and unsightliness in the garden.

Tying in Ramblers
It is possible that there are last year's new growths on the ramblers still remaining to be tied in. This should have of course been done last autumn, but if for any reason, it has not, there should be no more delay, because otherwise buds will be damaged in tying the shoots up and soon the loose canes will become almost unmanageable.

Checking Labels

There are some rose enthusiasts who label meticulously all their roses, so that they can be identified easily. No doubt this is an excellent idea. Early spring is the time to check the existing ones and to label permanently the plants that have been put in during the winter.

Mulching

After feeding, pruning and fighting pests and diseases, mulching is the most important item in the maintenance programme. Although in more recent times shredded polythene has been introduced as a satisfactory mulch, which has no humus content, and has to be removed from the beds at the end of the season, the primary objects of mulching are to supply humus to the soil and to conserve its moisture content during the warm sunny days. The more usual substances used for mulching therefore have a high humus content, and when they are ultimately dug into the soil in autumn they increase the moisture retention power of light soil and condition the heavier ones. These mulches are organic in character and are slowly decomposed, when they are spread on the beds, by the soil bacteria, producing plant nutrients and trace elements and also carbon dioxide, which is claimed by some authorities to be in sufficient concentration to assist the rose in producing its foods. Incidentally, it is also thought possible that, because they help to keep the roots moist, they check the progress of mildew. Although it is also believed by some rose growers that mulching has an effect on the incidence of black spot and rust, the evidence is not conclusive.

The time to mulch the ground is in May when the soil has warmed up. The mulch is spread in a layer at least two inches thick over the surface of the soil. This should be done when the earth is well wet after rain. All the weeds should be hoed out before doing so. There is no doubt that stable or farmyard manure is the ideal mulch, rather particularly because of its nutrient value, but in these days it is rather difficult to obtain. It has, however, one distinct disadvantage and this is that the birds tend to pick it off the beds and very untidily deposit it on the lawn, if the whole bed is covered with it. This can, however, be avoided if a margin of about 1 foot wide is left uncovered around the periphery of the beds. Usually the birds use this space for their antics instead of the lawn. Peat is an excellent mulch and source of humus, but it is expensive and has no nutrient value.

Well-made garden compost makes a very good mulch, especially if it contains a little fibrous material. It has the advantage of looking like soil, when it is spread, and has not the foreign appearance of some other mulching materials. Other suitable mulches are spent hops, leafmould and grass cuttings. Alternatively the beds can be mulched with a mixture of any of the organic substances mentioned above. Because of the risk of some heating up during the process of decomposition, particularly with grass cuttings, it is a wise precaution to leave a space around the base of the rose trees, when applying any mulch.

Application of Potash and Magnesium

It is beneficial to apply potassium sulphate and epsom salts at a rate of 2 ozs per square yard in the spring and fork it in. These are often absent, particularly in the lighter soils and the more chalky ones. Among other things, both these elements are concerned with the production of food in the plant and it is important to see that they are in good supply in the spring. It should, however, be remembered that these are the only two elements that should be put down individually. Any other plant foods should be put down in a correctly balanced mixture.

SUMMER

As the days lengthen and the summer arrives, the roses require continuous attention to keep them in good fettle. Fortunately most of these are not very onerous tasks and some can often be done in the course of a quiet stroll round the garden. Each of these are dealt with in more or less chronological order in the ensuing paragraphs.

Multiple Shoots

As the shoots grow in the late spring, often it will be found that three emerge from the same growing point. It is obvious that they are all competing with one another for nourishment. So if good strong shoots, with good foliage and flowers, are required, all but the largest of these should be removed. This can be done by rubbing out the unwanted ones with the thumb, if they have not grown too large. Although some roses have a greater propensity to develop multiply shoots, this is not a weakness in them, but nature's method of guarding against a mishap. After all her only interest is in producing seeds and reproducing her kind. If any rose stem is examined, it will be seen that at each leaf axil there are three potential shooting points. One in the centre, which is large and well developed and two others, which are only scars, far back in the wood on each side of it. These are undeveloped dormant eyes waiting to take over in an emergency. They are in fact termed 'guard' eyes. In many roses they never develop (Fig. 17).

Die-back

Another thing that should be looked out for quite early in the growing season is snags and shoots that have died back, perhaps due

FIG. 17. *Multiple Shoots*

Normally the two side shoots (A) are rubbed out with the thumb, but if the centre bud is damaged or too advanced (for exhibition purposes), one of the others may be retained

to frost damage. These should be removed because if they are not, the dead tissue might go back along the stalk to the union, and even into the root itself, in which case the plant would die.

Suckers

Sometimes when rose trees are growing, shoots rise from the ground that bear leaves that are different from the rest that are growing on them. This appearance is due to the fact that these are shoots emerging from the rootstock, and not the budded variety. If these are allowed to develop, they sap the strength of the rose itself. So as soon as they appear, the soil should be scraped away from the base of the rose and they should be torn away, pressing the soil down around the root with the foot so that this does not become damaged. They must on no account be cut away because this encourages the growth of a cluster of new shoots and the dormant 'guard' eyes to develop.

One of the possible causes of a rose throwing up suckers is faulty planting. Particular care should be taken, when doing so, to see that the union of the rose tree is well-bedded in the ground and that the roots go straight down into the soil. Stunted misplaced roots will produce suckers. Also it has been found that they can arise out of loose planting. Perhaps the only remedy in case of persistent suckering is to dig the roses up, while they are still comparatively young, remove all the growths and replant them correctly, preferably in fresh soil. This is, however, a rather drastic measure and is not very often necessary (Fig. 18).

Disbudding

This process is applied to hybrid tea roses and is something that is quite optional. Whether it is carried out depends largely upon the reader's taste. Some varieties have a tendency to bloom in small clusters, usually of three flowers. Others only produce a simple flower on each stem. The roses that have this propensity, usually have one main centre bud, which is well developed and on either side there are growing two smaller ones. Now if it is desired to have one large well-formed rose it is necessary to disbud, which means that, when each of the two secondary buds are about the size of a pea, they are picked off. If they are left on, flowers will develop, but, because of the competition for nourishment, not any of them would be as large as one developing alone would be. When specimen

Suckers (A), which are shown
in black, should be removed
by digging away the soil
and tearing, *not* cutting,
away at the roots at
points (B)

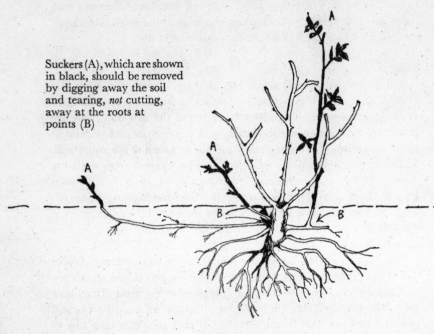

FIG. 18. *Suckers*

blooms are required for exhibition purposes disbudding is essential
(Fig. 19).

Before leaving this subject, attention must be drawn to the rise in
more recent years of a group of hybrid tea roses, which have a
strong tendency to grow their flowers on quite large heads if left
to go their own way. If these roses are disbudded they often produce
excellent specimen blooms, but if they are not, the flowers, that
develop on the numerous flowering stalks, are of a good average
size. Perhaps among the most outstanding of such varieties is
Pink Favourite, which has been seen to produce flower heads with
over 20 large well-formed roses. More recent introductions that have
a similar quality are Adair Roche, Pania and Silent Night, which
have been bred by the Northern Ireland rose hybridist, Sam
McGredy.

If this type of hybrid tea rose were developed to a larger extent, it
would be invaluable in the small garden of today, because it would

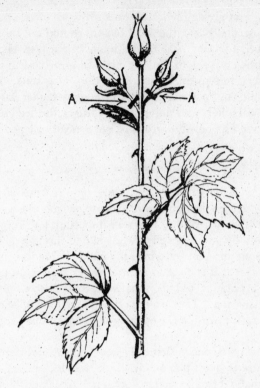

FIG. 19. *Disbudding*

The unwanted buds are picked off
at the points (A)

become possible to enjoy the delights of specimen hybrid teas and
floribundas with a limited number of bushes. In fact, in the extreme,
if there were only room for one rose tree in the garden, it could be
persuaded to produce both types at the same time!

Deadheading

This is the simple, but very essential, task of removing the dead
blooms from a rose tree. To do it efficiently, however, there are some
rules that must be obeyed. In the first place, it must be done
regularly. This is good for both the rose and the gardener. It

encourages and speeds up the next crop of flowers and it prevents the petals falling and giving the latter the hard work of tidying up the beds. In the second place, the dead blooms should not be cut with long stems because they bear the all-important leaves. Hybrid tea roses should be cut back to the first outward-growing leaf with five leaflets. If this does mean having an unduly long stalk, then it is probably judicious to remove the flower at a higher bud. With floribundas and other types that grow in clusters, the head should be removed at the first outward-growing eye beneath the pedicel.

Watering

If they are to be at their best, roses require copious supplies of water. So during a dry summer in order to get good roses, artificial watering must be carried out. It is very important for beginners not to be put off by the wise guys who, either through laziness or ignorance, maintain that watering only makes the roots come to the surface, or, that if it is done at all, tap water is harmful and rain-water must always be used. To start with, there is no evidence that the latter is true at all. The former possibly is, but it will be observed that the operative word in the opening sentence of this paragraph is 'copious'.

There is some evidence that only between 0.2 and 0.3% of the water taken in by most plants is used, the rest is dispersed through transpiration. So it can be seen to keep a rose tree flourishing during a very dry spell it must be given quite large quantities of water. Casual sprinkling for this reason is a waste of time.

When watering roses it is important because of the possible incidence of the fungus diseases, black spot, rust and mildew, to avoid as far as possible wetting the leaves because, if this is done, it can, if the temperature conditions happen to be right, encourage their development. With mildew, there is some evidence that it develops on a rose when the roots become dry. So when watering roses, it is important to use a method that will supply the soil with adequate quantities of moisture without wetting the leaves. Incidentally from a more aesthetic point of view, it is also undesirable to wet the blooms because they soon become blemished, particularly if they are exposed to the hot sun while they are still wet.

The best equipment to use for watering rose beds is a perforated plastic hose. This can be interwoven among the roses, and, if it is turned upside down so that the water penetrates directly into the soil, the foliage of the trees never gets wetted. Water can be run on a bed for several hours at a time without any inconvenience and if it is not a large one, sufficient water can be supplied to meet the needs of its occupants without changing the position of the hose. After watering, if the bed has not been mulched, the top soil should be lightly hoed to prevent rapid evaporation of the moisture. (See Fig. 20).

Weed Suppression

During the warmer months, particularly when the weather is wet, weeds develop very rapidly. If the beds are not too numerous, they

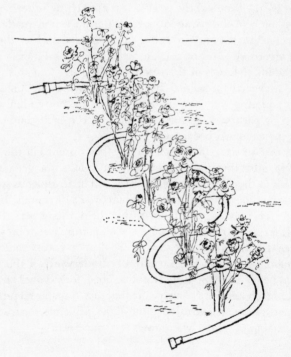

FIG. 20. *Watering Roses*

A perforated hose is turned upside down and interwoven among the bushes. In this way, wetting the leaves and blooms is avoided

can be kept free of these menaces fairly easily by regularly hoeing, but it must be done regularly otherwise they grow so fast that clearing them becomes a major operation. Mulching is a very affective weapon against weeds. Although it does not keep the beds completely free from them, the rate of their growth is so considerably curbed that they can be periodically chopped off with a hoe. When one considers all the other advantages of mulching it is probably the best way of dealing with weeds in a small garden.

Nowadays, however, there are very effective chemical methods of eradicating weeds available. Although these save a considerable amount of labour, they are of course a more expensive means of keeping weeds at bay. There are on the market today, under various trade names, two main chemicals that are used for this purpose. One is paraquat and the other is simazine. The first acts by being absorbed by the leaves of the weeds. It is applied by watering them with a solution of the paraquat preparation in water, made up to the maker's instructions, in spring and summer, when they are growing vigorously. It is important to see that the solution does not fall on the lower leaves of the rose trees. In order that this can be avoided, a specially designed sprinkler bar, which fits on to any ordinary watering can, can be used. There are no residual effects produced by paraquat, because as soon as it comes in contact with the soil, the chemical is denatured.

In the case of simazine preparations, they do not kill the weeds themselves, after they have developed, but inhibit the germination of the seeds in the soil. It is applied to the soil in an aqueous solution prepared in accordance with the manufacturer's directions. In their case, however, they are put down during the dormant period in the winter. It is essential to clear the beds of all mature weeds previously and to see that the soil at the time of application is very moist. The surface of the soil must remain unbroken afterwards if this weedkiller is to be effective. So it must not be hoed, forked over or raked. Rose growers should particularly note that there are special products, which have a low concentration of the active principle, for rose beds. It is essential to use these where roses are concerned.

The Care of Leaves

During the summer months there are a number of ways, in which the leaves of rose trees can be damaged or be detached, e.g. by pests, diseases, poor feeding (chlorosis), scorching by spraying or watering in the hot sun, fertilizers falling on them as a result of careless distribution, cutting too long stems when deadheading or gathering the flowers and so on. The leaves are so important to any plant that it is a vital necessity to give them the maximum protection at all times during the growing season. Not only are they the seat of the plant's food manufacturing processes, but, in addition, when they fade in autumn, they are responsible for the production of certain vital hormone substances, which are known as auxins. The function of these substances is to stimulate and control growth.

Fighting Pests and Diseases

These are vitally important tasks, which probably rank as the two most arduous in the summer maintenance programme. These are both dealt with fully in Chapters 12 and 13 respectively.

AUTUMN AND WINTER

Cutting Back in Autumn

In view of the fact that many present-day bush roses grow so tall, it is a good plan to cut their stems back to half their length in mid-autumn, so that the trees will not be rocked by strong winds and become loosened in the soil. The new first year wood on floribundas should be exceptions to this practice because as has already been discussed, these shoots should only be pruned lightly. Strong winds not only disturb the roots, but also cause a small hole in the soil at the base of the plant, in which water might collect and freeze when the frost comes. This could cause severe damage to the union. At the same time as this autumn pruning is carried out, all dead and diseased wood should be removed so as to reduce the work of pruning later in the winter.

Consolidating the Soil Around Rose Trees in Winter

In addition to strong winds, frost and excessive rain might loosen roses in the winter. In consequence, they should all be inspected regularly and firmed up when necessary by gently treading in the soil around them.

Winter Protection of Roses

Gardeners in Britain are singularly fortunate in one respect, when compared with those who live in the colder districts of Europe and the Northern states of America. In these places, it is necessary to protect rose bushes against the rigours of the severe winters by heaping soil up 10 inches or more over them. Standards have to be carefully laid down in trenches, without digging up the lower roots, and entirely buried. Sometimes in addition the branches of evergreens and leaves are piled on top of them to give even more protection. This is mentioned because there could be a small number of people in this country who live in excessively exposed parts and suffer high losses among their roses during winter. It might be worth their while to limit their activities to growing bushes and to protect them in this manner.

CHAPTER ELEVEN

Renovation of Old Roses and Rose Beds

Often one of the great problems that faces anybody who moves into a house, that has been previously occupied, is how to resuscitate the garden, which might have been badly neglected over some years and have become almost a wilderness. Among many other things, that need attention, are the rose beds. Having this problem might equally as well apply, when taking over a newly built house, because, owing to the shortage of building land in these days, new dwellings are sometimes erected in the grounds of older property. Even if the plot is well-kept, part of this old garden could easily contain some old rose beds, which are filled with plants, the condition of which ranges from flourishing to nearly dying. It is not really necessary to say so, but buying a house and moving in is a very expensive business in these days, and very often there is little money available initially to spend on the garden. It is necessary therefore to make do at least for the time being. As far as old roses are concerned it is possible to rejuvenate them without a lot of work within a year or two. They would then probably go on giving a considerable amount of joy for quite a long time. Among the very pleasing features of renovating old roses is that it makes it possible to enjoy in the garden some of the rather beautiful older varieties that are seldom seen in present-day rose-growers' catalogues.

Renovating Old Rose Bushes

When commencing the task of rejuvenating old rose bushes, the first thing to do is to look at the occupants of the beds and assess from their general state of health and appearance, the chances of their becoming useful plants. Very often, because their pruning has been neglected for many years in the past, or done badly, most of them consist of one or two, perhaps three, rather sinister looking bare, thick trunks, bearing many very ugly and fierce-looking thorns. Perhaps they are growing like this up to a height of about 2 feet. From their upper extremities there might emanate a bevy of young, healthy shoots, which have relatively good foliage and perhaps some quite colourful flowers. If this growth is supported by just a single basal stem, they are rather like slightly undersized, but neglected, half standards. In this condition they are quite unsuitable for beds. On the other hand, some of the occupants of the bed might be obviously dead, while others look as if they are fast waning. It is quite evident that these must be replaced. This must not, however, be done immediately because, for the reasons given later in this chapter, the soil in which roses have been growing for a long time, say, some ten or more years, will not sustain new roses satisfactorily.

Turning to the question of how to treat the old roses that have good prospects of living, while there is a good chance of making them all into good bushes, the ones, which have more than one stout branch growing from the ground, have the greatest hope of being reclaimed. The procedure is a drastic one, that consists of cutting down the old shoots to a lower dormant eye, when the weather is open during the winter, in the hope that the bush will shoot afresh from these growing points. In most cases this desire is fulfilled. In doing this, there are two things that must be remembered. The first is that after so many years with very little interference, this action will be quite a shock to the trees. The second is that if all these old stems are cut down at the same time, it will be quite late in the following season before there is any substantial amount of foliage on the trees. This might be detrimental to them when they are en-deavouring to re-establish themselves, because, as is known, the leaves are vital to the life of any plant. It is better therefore to spread the cutting back over two, or even three years, if there are more than two basal shoots. In each successive year, one stout stem should be pruned back to a low dormant eye. This will leave the younger shoots on the one or two other branches to produce leaves in sufficient quantity to ensure that the health of the rose is not impaired. In the following year, another of the older shoots is tackled in a similar way. Such action minimises the shock at a vital moment in the rose's lifetime. In such cases where there is only one stout stem, this must of course be pruned in this way, and a chance must be taken on the survival of the bush.

The best tool to use for this work is a sharp pruning knife, or, if the stems are very tough, a pruning saw. As a preliminary all the dead and diseased wood and the weak twigs should be removed. Then the selected branch is cut with an upward cut towards the side of the stem on which the dormant bud is situated. This should, of course, be just above it. In order that the bark is not torn or damaged in any way, the top growth is held in the left hand so that its weight is supported when the cutting is done. The open wound should be finally covered with lead paint to protect it. The dormant eye on an old rose is not always easily discernible, but careful examination will reveal it. Generally it is only a very small bud, like a small pip, in a scar on the surface of the bark. After pruning is completed, the soil in the bed should be well fertilized, preferably with farmyard manure.

Replacing Roses in Old Rose Beds – Rose Sickness

As suggested previously, a great mistake is often made by enthusiastic gardeners on finding that some of the roses in an old rose bed need replacing, when they rush out and buy replacements and plant them right away in the same places as the old ones stood. Probably the new occupants will live, at least for a time, but they will look decidedly seedy. Instead of their older wood being a fresh green colour, it tends to die back. Any new growth that appears from the base of the tree will be very weak. The plant will be so miserable that the gardener will be most dissatisfied and perhaps develop a minor grudge against his supplier. If he ultimately digs it up, he would find that any roots that had developed, were just below the soil surface. They would be mainly fibrous and emerging high up on the main stem, with only a few growing lower down. Any tap-roots that had developed would be stunted and most likely rotten. One thing that is vitally important at this stage is for the gardener, thinking he has bought some inferior stock, not to replace such roses with still more new ones, because there is real trouble present and it must be dealt with right away. The reason for the failure of new roses planted in old rose beds is that the soil is suffering from rose 'sickness', which is a condition that develops if it has been accommodating roses for ten or more years.

Actually nobody is quite sure what is the reason for this happening, but there are a number of theories, which will be discussed later on in this chapter. In the meantime, it is important to tell the practical gardener what he should do in order that he can be sure that any new roses with which he replaces the old worn-out ones will flourish. In the first place, when all of them need changing and the beds can be cleared, to obtain quick results, the best thing to do is to replace all the old soil, to a depth of 15 inches, with some that has either been taken from elsewhere in the garden or bought in from the outside. In both cases, it is imperative to be absolutely sure that roses have never been grown in it before. When, however, the occupants of the bed have only to be partially replaced, it is advisable to dig a hole at least 12 inches deep and eighteen inches square for each new rose bush, and to fill it with soil from another part of the garden, where roses have not been grown previously. Fortunately the soil that is excavated in either case, may be deposited anywhere else in the garden, providing the site is not intended for roses. Other crops will come to no harm if planted in it.

If, for any reason, replacing the soil in a bed is physically impossible, or suitable new supplies are not easily obtainable, a green crop, such as mustard, can be grown in the bed and repeatedly dug in for two years. Alternatively grass seed can be sown in the bed, but in this case it should be laid under grass for three years before any roses are put into it again. If there is space available, and the layout of the garden permits it, the easiest thing to do is to cut new beds in the lawn some feet away from the original ones and to use the turves removed to grass the latter over after they have been levelled. As mentioned on page 64, it is a good plan to make provision for this ultimate movement when the beds are originally laid out.

Why does Soil become 'Rose' Sick?

As mentioned above, there are a number of theories that have been advanced to explain this phenomenon, but nobody fully knows what rose 'sickness' is or what causes it. Perhaps one of the more puzzling aspects of this soil condition is that the old established roses, that have been well looked after, if left undisturbed, do not suffer from it, whereas new replacements planted in exactly the same positions will soon deteriorate. It could be that the former have strong tap-roots that can search out all the needs of the plant in more distant parts, where the source of trouble has not penetrated.

One theory that has been advanced is that the breaking away of root hairs and their deposits cause toxins to be formed in the soil and these poison any other plants of the same genus that are planted in the vicinity. This does not appear at first sight to be a very satisfactory explanation, but it is certainly one that has been put forward. Another suggestion is that the trace elements in the soil have become exhausted after this long time to such a large extent that it is not possible to replace them by ordinary fertilization.

In more recent years, research workers have suggested that this condition is brought about principally by the soil being overrun by eelworms or *nematodes*. These microscopic creatures, it is explained, eat away the root hairs and bore into the cell tissues of the roots of the new roses and steal the plant's food after it has been manufactured. As a result the young bushes are weakened to such an extent that they die in the following winter because during the dormant period they have to rely on the nutriment that normally is available in the roots to keep them going. Even this theory does not explain completely why old roses will still flourish in this infected soil unless their root system and other food stores are so large and well-developed that they can provide enough food to keep both the eelworms and themselves going. On the other, the roots of older plants might be so tough that the nematodes cannot penetrate them.

Although it is not absolutely conclusive, perhaps the fact that methods, that are designed to destroy eelworms in the soil, appear to renew its ability to sustain new roses in old rose beds, must be accepted as supporting evidence for this theory. In the first place it has been found that steam sterilization of the soil is quite effective against these minute pests. This unfortunately can only be carried out on the soil in glasshouses on a nursery, where supplies of steam are available on a commercial scale. Another very effective method of control, which is applicable to open ground, but which is not very suitable for amateur gardeners to undertake, is the use of the chemical fumigant, carbon disulphide, which has such a vile smell that it would be nearly impossible to use in a private garden with nearby neighbours. It is however, referred to here because it does give some support to the belief that eelworms or some other minute organisms are responsible for rose 'sickness' of soil.

Fumigation with this chemical is carried out on a bed, emptied of its roses. Holes are bored in the soil with a broom handle, about 9 inches deep and 3 feet apart all over the bed. In each hole is poured about 3½ fluid ounces of carbon disulphide and then it is sealed off by treading in the soil at its entrance. In a very short time all the organisms present are destroyed. If any amateur is tempted to carry out this procedure, he should be warned that this chemical is very explosive and should not be stored near a naked flame, or put down when smoking. There are in addition several other chemicals sold to commercial growers for the purpose of destroying eelworms, but these are not available to amateur gardeners. Some more recent research has been carried out that indicates that certain fungi destroy eelworms in the soil. If cultures of these could be made to grow in the soil, perhaps this might lead to safe methods of dealing with these minute creatures and overcome rose 'sickness'.

There is in addition another aspect of rose 'sickness' that must be discussed before this subject is dropped. It is well known that roses derive some of their supplies of nitrogen from the atmosphere through the agency of nitrogen fixing bacteria that convert it into nitrogenous food in a form that is readily assimilated by the plant. It is important therefore for the well-being of the plants that an adequate supply of atmospheric nitrogen is readily available in the soil. Now all soils after they have been dug up resettle. In the absence of such substances as humus and lime, the rate of settling is greater. Prolonged rain and melting snow hasten this consolidation still more. As a result the absorption of atmospheric nitrogen is lessened and the plants in turn suffer. It is possible therefore that rose 'sickness' of the soil in beds, where roses have been growing for a long time, is due to it becoming over-consolidated, particularly when the beds have been neglected. In addition, it is regarded as good gardening practice never to disturb the soil in rose beds to a greater depth than about 2 inches because of the risk of damaging their surface roots. Under these circumstances, when beds are very old, the soil is likely to become very compact. It is thought that this theory is one that might explain why very old roses are still able to flourish in old soil, whereas newly planted ones do not thrive. The established roses, that have strong, long roots, might be able to seek out the places, where the nitrogen is plentiful, and so maintain a good supply of this vital element to the plants, while the undeveloped ones of the newcomers can only operate in a limited local area, in which, following a long period of compaction, it takes this bacterial process some time to start up again. In the meantime, while it is getting into its stride, the newly planted roses have to struggle desperately for their existence.

If this theory is a true one, it is evident that in order to prevent rose 'sickness', everything must be done to be sure that the soil remains open and that it does not easily consolidate. This is not so easy once a bed has been made and planted out. It can, however, be assisted in two ways. The first is to maintain the pH of the soil between 5 and 6, because at this level, compaction appears to be lessened and any damaging effects arrested. It can also be minimised by making regular additions of humus in adequate quantities. This is probably done best by means of regular mulching. As prevention is better than cure, the chance of the soil becoming overcompacted, even if the beds are neglected over a long period, are considerably reduced if, firstly, large quantities of humus are incorporated, when the beds are first made and, secondly, in the case of a clay subsoil, it is conditioned by treating it with lime.

CHAPTER TWELVE

Modern Method of Fighting Pests

Roses in common with other plants are attacked by insect pests. These menaces are largely repulsed at the present time by means of toxic chemicals. These are very efficient as far as destroying them is concerned, but unfortunately they have been suspected for some time of having a deleterious effect on other forms of harmless wild life, which has become a matter of considerable concern. As a result, research work is being carried out currently with the object of finding alternative methods of control. This subject is dealt with in greater detail later in this chapter.

It is the organochlorine pesticides that have been thought to be particularly dangerous. Among these the very well known compound DDT has given most concern. This is because ideally any chemical, that is used in horticulture, should be automatically rendered harmless by the conditions of its environment immediately after it has fulfilled its specific purpose, but DDT is very persistent. Chemical analysis has shown its presence in the soil, long after it has been used, water supplies, the sea, in the bodies of birds and fish, the Antarctic snow, in the fat deposits in the human body and in a range of foodstuffs. Apart from some unconfirmed results of work on mice, there is no positive scientific evidence to date that DDT has any deleterious effect on birds and other forms of wild life. In addition, there is no record of any health hazards to human beings, even to those workers in industry, who are constantly exposed to concentration levels of DDT, that are far higher than are met in the normal way of living. Nevertheless authorities who are responsible for the health of the people, cannot fail to recognise such a persistent chemical as DDT, which must inevitably accumulate in the human system, as a potential danger, until it is established to be otherwise. In consequence, during the past few years, its use has been restricted in Arizona, Australia and Canada and banned in Norway, Denmark and the States of California and Michigan. Now, as the result of a report by the Advisory Committee on Pesticides and Other Toxic Chemicals, published in December

1969, it will be banned for gardening purposes and a number of other agricultural and horticultural uses in this country. Fortunately, as the Committee points out, there are other permissible organo-chlorines and also a number of organophosphorus chemicals, that can effectively replace it, so gardeners should in no way suffer. There is no doubt that when this ban becomes law, manufacturers will appropriately reformulate any of their products that contain DDT.

In addition, as a further precaution, gardeners can minimise the amount of spraying done by, wherever possible, using other methods of destruction, such as hand-picking caterpillars. To do the latter, in any case, is advantageous because simultaneously with their coming, the larvae of the ladybirds appear, which, while being harmless in themselves, are predators of aphides or greenflies. Spraying with insecticides kills them as well as the pests.

Insects that attack Roses

So that gardeners can wage war successfully against the principal rose pests, it is important for them to know a little about the insects that they are likely to encounter and to have some knowledge of the most modern and efficient weapons that can be employed against them.

There is quite a wide range of insects that menace roses, but fortunately only a small number of types are particularly common. Usually if these are effectively dealt with, most of the minor ones are destroyed simultaneously. It is important nevertheless that a gardener should have some idea of what these more rare insects look like and how they affect roses because it is always possible for a serious onslaught to take place. For this reason, some information of these lesser common insects are included in these pages.

Although entymologists divide the insects into a number of different classes, according to the differences in the characteristics of their anatomy, it is sufficient for the purpose of this book to limit the breakdown to two categories. The first of these contains all those pests that bite and chew their food (mandibulate). This class includes caterpillars, chafers, millepedes, sawflies, woodlice and some beetles. The other category covers the piercing and/or sucking insects (haustellate), that pierce or scrape the surface of the leaves and shoots and feed on the sap. The most important of these are aphides, capsid bugs, frog-hoppers (cuckoo spit insects), rose leaf-hoppers, thrips, red spider mites and scale insects or coccids.

Before giving the details that will help gardeners to recognise any of these pests, either by their appearance or by the devastation that they cause, and the specific insecticides that are used for their destruction, it is of value to consider for a little while the types of insecticides that are available and the manner in which they act. There are two varieties at present in use – the first are contact washes and the second are systemics. Up to fairly recently, all insecticides were of the former type. These have essentially to be sprayed on to the plants, when the pests have appeared, to be fully effective. They destroy, according to the type of insects treated, either by being absorbed in the stomach and poisoning them or through the respiratory system, resulting in their suffocation and the paralysis of their nervous system.

The more recent introduction of systemic insecticides has changed to some extent the techniques used in fighting pests. These toxins are sprayed on the foliage of the plants and are absorbed in the sap. Thus the toxic material is spread throughout the plant and acts as a very effective defence, particularly against the sap-sucking insects. This latter type of insecticide has marked advantages over the contact variety. One of the most beneficial of these to present-day gardener, is that it is usually only necessary to spray once in the spring, and to follow with another treatment, or at the most two, at monthly intervals. It is not necessary therefore to keep a constant vigil for the arrival of the successive waves of insects and to be constantly bringing out the spray as is the case with contact insecticides. There are several different chemicals in use for destroying pests. Those that are most commonly employed in this country at the present time are given below:—

Contact Insecticides: Derris, gamma – BHC (Lindane), Pyrethrum, Synergised Pyrethrum, Malathion.

Systemic Insecticides: Dimethoate, Menazon, Oxydemeton-methyl.

A number of these chemicals are sold under trade names. Some of these proprietary preparations are mixtures of both systemic and contact substances. They are thus of great value for spraying roses, on which the pests have already appeared and, at the same time, they protect them against future attacks.

Norris Pratt (Floribunda)
Deep Yellow.
Raised by Buisman, 1967

City of Leeds (Floribunda)
Rich Salmon.
Raised by McGredy, 1966

Satchmo (Floribunda)
Brilliant Red.
Raised by McGredy, 1970

Dr. Barnado (Floribunda)
Crimson
Raised by Harkness, 1969

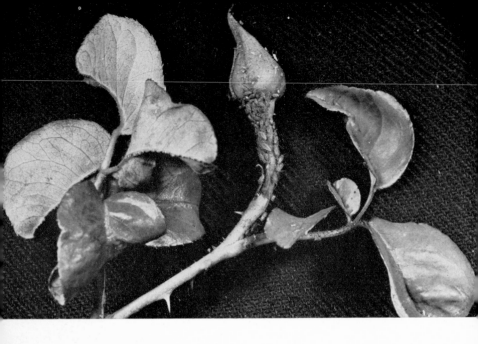

A rose infested with aphides (greenfly)

A rose attacked by thrips

Leaf-rolling rose sawfly

Sap-sucking Insects
Aphides (Greenflies)

Aphides are all too familiar to gardeners for it to be necessary to give them a detailed description. The commonest species appearing on roses is *Macrosiphum rosae* L. Perhaps it should, however, be mentioned that they are not always green in colour. They can also be pink, red or brown. They breed very rapidly and roses can become infested with them within a few hours.

Because they suck the sap from the plants, they have the effect of reducing their vigour, and as a result the leaves fall. The shoots are crippled and the leaves become distorted. Apart from their direct deleterious effect, there are two side reactions to their activities, that make them a very serious menace. Firstly, they exude on to the leaves a sweet sticky fluid, honeydew, which is an ideal growing medium for the fungus, Sooty Mildew; secondly, they are carriers of virus diseases. It is imperative therefore that prompt action is taken to destroy them.

They are easily eradicated by spraying with contact or systemic insecticides (See page 135). It should, however, be mentioned that greenflies have a certain number of natural enemies, among which are tits and sparrows, ladybirds and their larvae, the larvae of hover-flies and of lace-wing flies and certain parasites that live on their hosts internally. It is, however, necessary in some seasons to supplement the predatory efforts of these insects with chemicals because of their late appearance, when the weather conditions are not suitable to them. It should also be noted that excessive feeding of nitrogen makes the shoots soft and they thus become an easy prey to these menaces.

Rose Thrips (Thunder- or Blackflies)

There are a number of species of thrips that attack garden plants, but the one that primarily menaces roses is *Thrips fuscipennis* Hal. The adult insects are long and narrow, about $\frac{1}{16}$ inches in length, and are black or dark brown in colour. They have two pairs of narrow wings and bead-like antennae. They lay their eggs within the tissues of the outer petals at the time when the calyx starts to open out and in those of the foliage and shoots. The damage is done by the nymphs, immature thrips, which are similar in appearance to their parents, but are pale to reddish-yellow in colour, smaller

E

and wingless. They lacerate and break up the tissue and feed on the pulped material.

When roses are affected, the presence of these insects is obvious. The leaves are mottled in appearance, the young shoots are mal-formed and the petals are damaged, when the buds develop.

They are dealt with by spraying with insecticides (See page 135).

Capsid Bugs (Lygus pabulinus L.)

These insects, which appear as small green wingless nymphs in spring, feed by boring into the tissues of the leaves and extracting the sap.

When they have been attacked by this pest, the leaves, flower buds and tips of the shoots of the roses are distorted. Often there are dark brown areas appearing on the leaves, which are sometimes erro-neously thought to be due to black spot.

For methods of eradication, see page 135.

Rose Leaf-hoppers (Typhlocyba rosae L.)

The adults are very energetic pale yellowish hoppers that jump and fly. Once again, it is the almost colourless nymphs that do the damage by sucking the sap. They are hatched from eggs that have been laid in groups of up to four beneath the skin of the leaves.

The leaves of roses, when attacked, get a mottled appearance and drop early. Growth is also checked.

Early measures should be taken against these pests by spraying the undersides of the leaves, where the insects act, with systemic or contact insecticides (See page 135). A second brood occurs in late August and September so similar steps should be taken then to destroy them.

Frog-hoppers (Cuckoo-spit Insects)

These are yellowish-green insects which surround themselves with the frothy or spittle-like mass, which makes them so familiar to gardeners. The species that affects roses is known as *Philaenus leucophthalmus* L. .

The adults, which are active, jumping and flying insects, varying in colour from pale yellow, through shades of brown to black, do little damage to plants.

The nymphs feed by sucking the sap resulting in the wilting of the flower buds and the shoots and the bending of the tender growths.

There is a tendency for climbers to be more heavily affected than bushes.

The insects are destroyed by spraying with insecticides (See page 135), using a forceful spray, so that the frothy envelope that surrounds them is broken up. Although it is rather a messy business, spraying can be avoided by hand-picking the insects.

Scale Insects (Coccids)

The shoots and stems of roses are sometimes encrusted with scale insects, of which Scurfy Scale, *Aulacaspis rosae* Bouché, is the most common. The stems are covered with round flat whitish scales, which are the female insects and smaller elongated white scales – the males. The eggs are laid beneath this scaly covering. From these the nymphs, which are orange-coloured are hatched. They then crawl out and wander for a time over the shoots, giving the plant the appearance of having been dusted with red pepper. Eventually each nymph settles in one position and feeds by sucking the sap from the plant, the growth of which is seriously retarded. As the nymphs age, they turn whitish in colour.

To eradicate this pest, timely action must be taken in the autumn when the insects are in the nymphal stage. They should be sprayed with an insecticide (See page 136), using a high pressure spray.

Red Spider Mites (*Tetranychus telarius* L.)

These pests, which have long been a menace to roses grown under glass, are increasingly turning their attention to outdoor roses in this country. They are so minute in size, rarely longer than about 0.01 inch long, that they can only be seen with a magnifying glass. They are difficult to detect because they live and breed on the lower surface of the leaves, which are enmeshed in a fine silken web. They are often mistaken for specks of dust because they are so immobile that it is difficult to tell whether they are alive or dead.

Their presence is detected by their effect on the leaves, which become mottled and generally off-colour. In severe infestations, the latter become yellow and fall off prematurely. The vigour of the rose-trees attacked is reduced and they often become prone to winter damage.

Red Spider Mites have a short stiff spine on the top of the jaw, with which they pierce the epidermis of the plant, and extract the sap.

There has been experienced considerable difficulty in controlling them over the years because these insects have readily built up a resistance to a succession of insecticides, that were initially very effective. It is known however, that they hibernate on weeds and in the cracks in the bark of bushes and supporting stakes. In the consequence, the first step in control is to destroy anything possible that might harbour them. The plants should be sprayed with the insecticides given on page 136.

Leaf-eating Insects (including Leaf-rolling Insects)
Caterpillars
There is a wide range of caterpillars, which are of course the larvae of various moths, that devastate roses. The different types of injury caused by them, together with the insects that are responsible are given in the table below:—

Defoliation, partial or full	The larvae of the following moths: Buff Tip (*Phalera bucephala L.*), Lackay (*Malacosoma neustria L.*), Vapourer (*Orgyia antiqua L.*), and Winter (*Operophtera brumata L.*).
Leaf-rolling	Tortrix moth larvae or Rose Maggots.
Bud or flower injury	Tortrix moth larvae or Rose Maggots.
Leaf-skeletonising	The larvae of Yellow-Tail (*Euproctis chrysorrhoea L.*), and Buff Tip Moths.

The leaf-rolling larvae are the most difficult to deal with because they roll themselves up in the leaves and so protect themselves against any insecticide spray. They are best dealt with by looking out for them early in the spring and hand-picking them. If it becomes a very heavy infestation it is necessary however to use insecticides. The latter should be, however, avoided as far as possible because often the ladybirds and their larvae and other predators of aphides are destroyed at the same time (See page 136).

Sawflies
Although roses are attacked by about twenty species of sawflies, the most serious are the large rose sawfly (*Arge ochropus Gmel.*), the leaf-rolling sawfly (*Blennocampa pusilla Klug*), and the Rose Slug Sawfly (*Endelomyia aethiops F.*).

The Large Sawfly

The larvae of this sawfly is bluish-green and yellowish-black along the back and has six rows of black shining bristle-bearing tubercles. Below these over the legs is a large shining black spot which has several bristles. The adult lays its egg in a double row on the shoots, making a separate incision for each egg. This becomes blackened and indicates the presence of these insects.

The Leaf-rolling Rose Sawfly

The adults are black shining insects, with expansive wings, not unlike winged Queen Ants in appearance. They lay their eggs in May or early June in the marginal area of the leaves under the leaf-tissue. During the laying of eggs, the female injects a toxic substance and this causes the leaf to roll. It then serves to protect the larvae, which hatch out some days later, and also to provide them with food.

This rolling effect makes it difficult to attack these insects by spraying. After rolling has taken place, the best thing to do is to hand-pick the leaves and burn them. As a precautionary measure, the plant, however, may be sprayed with an insecticide in May in order to deter the female from laying her eggs. In gardens that are overshadowed by trees, this is a good thing to do as a routine, because under such conditions attacks appear to be prevalent (See page 136).

The Rose Slug Sawfly

The adults are black shining insects. They usually make two appearances during the growing season. The first is between the middle of May and the middle of June. The second is in July and August. They lay their eggs in the serrations on edges of the young leaves, usually they put one egg within each leaf. The larvae are yellowish in colour, but they assume a greenish hue, because the green food in the alimentary canal can be seen through their skin. Unless they are in deep shade, when they devour both surfaces these insects feed on the upperside of the leaves, leaving the upper skin unharmed. The damaged leaves are skeletonised and after a time, they dry up and turn brown and have a scorched appearance. To control these pests both surfaces of the leaves should be sprayed with an insecticide (See page 136).

Leaf-cutter Beetles

These are very irritating pests, because the females cause considerable disfigurement by cutting out large oblong and circular pieces from the leaves, which they use to make their nests and there is little that one can do about it, except catch them in nets when they are savaging a plant, or find their nest and destroy it.

Root-eating Pests
Chafer Beetles

There are four species of chafers that affect roses. They are the Cockchafer or 'May Bug', *Melolontha melolontha* L., the Rose Chafer, *Cetonia aurata* L., the Garden Chafer or 'Bracken Clock', *Phyllopertha horticola* L., and the Summer Chafer, *Amphimallon solstitialis* L. The incidence of the latter is rather less than that of the other three insects. The adults of all these insects feed on the foliage, flower buds and blooms of roses and the larvae remain in the soil and devour the young roots.

The Cockchafer

This is a large beetle with a black head and thorax, reddish-brown, slightly hairy wing cases, on each of which there are five raised parallel lines. The tip of the antennae is clubbed. The larvae ('White Grub' or 'Joe Bassett', as they are called), are a dirty white colour, thick and fleshy with the last segments of the abdomen enlarged and coloured dark-purplish brown. They are about $1\frac{1}{2}$ inches long. These insects are prevalent in light sandy soil.

The Rose Chafer

This insect is distinguished from the Cockchafer by being smaller and having metallic, bright golden green coloured wing cases and thorax. The wing cases have white spots all over them. Its grubs are very similar in appearance to those of the cockchafer, but their bodies have rows of reddish hair.

The Garden Chafer

This is the smallest of the four chafers described here. It is from $\frac{1}{3}$ to $\frac{1}{2}$ inch in length. The thorax has a bluish-green hue and the wing cases are reddish-brown. The larvae are like that of the Cockchafer beetle, but they are proportionately reduced in size. The garden chafer is distinguished from the first two described by the fact that, when adult, it flies in bright sunshine, instead of at dusk, which is the characteristic time for the other two to appear.

The Summer Chafer

This insect is about $\frac{2}{3}$ inch long. It is reddish brown in colour and has a rather more lanky body than a garden chafer.

All these insects are eradicated by spraying them with an insecticide (see page 136) as soon as they appear. Hoeing the soil will often throw up their grubs, when, if the birds do not get them first, they should be collected and destroyed.

If chafer beetle grubs are troublesome in an established bed of roses they can be exterminated by making four holes, about 1 inch in diameter, in the soil, at the points of the compass around each rose tree and pouring into each about $\frac{1}{3}$ fluid ounce of the very highly inflammable chemical, carbon disulphide, and sealing each hole by treading in the soil at its mouth. If, however, this rather drastic step is taken, the neighbours should be warned to keep their windows closed because this compound has a vile smell.

MODERN INSECTICIDES

PESTS	CONTACT PREPARATION CONTAINING:	COMBINED SYSTEMIC AND CONTACT PROPRIETARY MIXTURES OF:
Aphides:	Derris, gamma-BHC (Lindane) Malathion, Pyrethrum, Synergised Pyrethrum	(1) Menazon/gamma – BHC (2) Dimethoate/DDT* (3) Dimethoate/Malathion/DDT (4) Oxydemeton-methyl
Thrips:	As for Aphides	(1) Menazon/gamma–BHC (2) Dimethoate/DDT (3) Dimethoate/Malathion/DDT
Capsid Bugs:	As for Aphides	As for Thrips
Rose Leaf-hoppers:	As for Aphides	As for Thrips
Frog-hoppers (Cuckoo Spit Insects):	As for Aphides	As for Thrips

CONTACT	COMBINED SYSTEMIC AND CONTACTS
Scale Insects (Coccids):	
Malathion. 3% Tar Oil Wash (in December)	As for Thrips
Red Spider Mites:	
(5) Petroleum White Oil Emulsion (during the summer) Tar Oil Winter Wash to destroy eggs (in winter)	(4) Oxydemeton-methyl (during the summer)
Caterpillars:	
As for Aphides	As for Thrips
Sawfly-Slug:	
As for Aphides	As for Thrips
Leaf-rolling:	
As for Aphides, but all applied when the adult leaf-rolling sawflies are seen in the vicinity before the leaves roll	As for Thrips
Chafer Beetles:	
Malathion, Pyrethrum, Synergised Pyrethrum	As for Thrips
Chafer Beetles Larvae:	
See page 135 (as under Aphides on p. 135.)	

---

(1)   Abol. X – Plant Protection Ltd.
(2)   Systemic Insecticide (Murphy) – Murphy Chemical Co. Ltd.
(3)   Pestex – Fisons Horticultural Ltd.
(4)   Metasystox Aphid Gun - Baywood Chemicals Ltd.
(5)   Volck

Author's Note
   Because of new legislation ultimately barring DDT as a garden insecticide, it is anticipated that manufacturers will have reformulated their preparations by 1972 so as to replace it with less toxic compounds. Currently there is no restriction on the remaining chemicals in the above list.

Modern Research Work on the Elimination of Pests

Earlier in this chapter, it was stated that a description of some of the work, that is being carried out to find alternative methods to spraying for the destruction of unwanted pests, would be given.

The Search for New Selective Insecticides

The scientists, who are working in this field, are looking for toxic chemicals that will limit their destructive action to specified harmful insects. At first sight this may seem to be a tall order, but actually it is not such a difficult one because something similar has already been achieved in closely related spheres of pest extermination. The first example of this is the case of the very old established rodenticide, red squill, which is deadly poisonous to mice and rats, but which has hardly any effect on dogs and cats. This selective action against rodents is due to the fact that these animals have below average vomiting powers, whereas cats and dogs are endowed with very efficient emetic abilities and in consequence are able to dispose of the poison readily, if they happen to eat it.

Turning to insects, house-flies, that have become immune to the effect of DDT, afford an excellent example of specificity in insecticides. As a result of their research work, scientists in recent years have discovered that a chemical, N-di-n-butyl-p-chlorobenzene, when mixed with it, has the power to enhance the effectiveness of unboosted DDT against such flies. This synergised DDT, as it is termed, has proved to be specific in its action in this respect.

Another interesting case of specificity is that of the well-known insecticide, malathion, which, while it destroys insects, is harmless to domestic pets. This selectivity is due to the different manner in which this chemical is broken down in the insect and animal bodies. Actually malathion itself is non-poisonous, but, when absorbed by both insects and animals, it is converted into another compound, malaoxon, which is deadly poisonous to both. In the case of insects, however, the reaction takes place so fast that a lethal dose is built up very rapidly. On the other hand, in the animal metabolism, the rate of production is so slow that the malaoxon is broken down by further metabolic action before it can do any harm. Thus malathion is a specific poison for insects.

This knowledge suggests a possible approach to this problem. If scientists can discover chemicals that are discriminate in their action between the various species of insects, this would go a long way towards the development of methods of destroying exclusively pests, without harming other forms of harmless wild-life. To achieve this objective, further research will be necessary into the toxological and morphological differences that exist among the many insects, both friends and foes, that exist in nature.

Recent Research on Techniques for Eradicating Pests

Another aspect of the extermination of insect pests, that is receiving considerable attention from scientists, is the development of new techniques, that do not involve the use of toxins on the present widespread scale. For sometime it has been known that insects exude hormone compounds, which are known as pheromones, that are designed either to repel or attract other insects. The research work that has so far been done suggests that such compounds with sex attractant properties might provide an excellent field of specificity in the destruction of pests. Examples of such insects that are known to have this characteristic are the queen bee, the cockroach, wireworm and cabbage-hopper. It is evident that if these attractant hormones could be extracted or synthesised in sufficient quantities they could be used to bait traps to capture specific insects, which then could be destroyed under controlled conditions without the broad dissemination of the toxic insecticides.

Hitherto, such compounds have been found difficult to isolate and identify, which are two essential steps if they are to be synthesised in large enough quantities for this purpose. Recently, however, it has been found that the virgin female wireworm, *Limonius californicus* secretes a sex pheromone, which has been identified as valeric acid, which is a comparatively simple compound. Further research along these lines, might reveal that other garden pests exude similar easily synthesised compounds and this might lead to this method of pest eradication becoming a very satisfactory means of overcoming many present-day difficulties.

Control of Male Fecundity as a Method of Pest Destruction

Recent scientific research has produced two methods that might be of great future use in the control of pests. Both of these are specific in their action. The first has already been tried out and proved very successful in the elimination of some insect scourges in various parts of the world. In both the methods described below, the principle is the same. The males of an obnoxious species, that are bred in captivity, are rendered sterile and then released in an infested area to consort with the wild females. Their unproductive mating results in local suppression, or even eradication, of the species.

In the first of these two techniques, which is the one that has already been used in large scale insect control, the process is to expose the males to nuclear irradiation, which sterilises them. There is, however, one weakness in this method, which manifests itself in the case of species that mate more than once in a season. While there is an excellent chance of a female having intercourse with a sterile male in the first instance, later in the season she might meet up with a wild untreated partner and reproduction would take place. The second method, which was developed about two years ago, however, should overcome this difficulty. This arises from the synthesis of a hormone-like chemical, which has all the characteristics of juvenile hormone, which is the natural substance, that occurs in insects, that is concerned with controlling larvae development. This synthetic hormone has three properties, which enables its use as a pest eradicant. These are that (1) if larvae come in contact with it, the normal process is interfered with and the chrysalis fails to develop, (2) if adult males are contaminated with it and are afterwards allowed to mate, the resulting issue fail to mature and (3) males so treated transfer a minute quantity of this chemical to the female at the time of intercourse and they in turn are rendered permanently non-fertile. Hence it will be seen that the chance of later breeding in the case of species that mate more than once in a season is minimised. The procedure in this method is quite simple. Males reared in captivity are exposed to this synthetic hormone and released to mingle with the wild females.

Controlled Distribution of Predators as Method of Pest Eradication

It has already been mentioned that certain insects, such as ladybirds and their larvae, the larvae of hover-flies and so on are the natural enemies of aphides. The controlled breeding and release of such insects affords to scientists another line of approach to this problem of destroying harmful insects without injuring other forms of wild life. Recently, in fact, ladybirds have been bred in captivity at a research station in France and released in areas, in which these very destructive insects are rife. Neither ladybirds nor their larvae do any harm to plants or other forms of wild life and therefore have none of the dangers that are inherent in the toxic sprays that are now so commonly used.

Breeding Plants that are Immune to Pests

The genetic approach to the lessening of destruction of garden plants and crops is another aspect of this problem that is receiving the active attention of scientists. This is a field that is viewed quite hopefully, particularly as there has already been considerable success along these lines in the breeding of disease-resistant strains. This undoubtedly will be a line of action which will be energetically followed because its success will not only eliminate any risk of danger to other forms of wild life, but, in addition, it will lessen the amount of energy that is dissipated by gardeners, nurserymen and farmers in the arduous task of regular spraying.

It is hoped that this brief outline of the ways in which chemists, botanists, entomologists, plant breeders and others are striving together to overcome this great problem, will reassure the many readers who are at the present time genuinely alarmed at the wide-reaching destruction that indiscriminate spraying with toxic chemicals might cause.

CHAPTER THIRTEEN

Modern Ways of Fighting Rose Diseases

Unfortunately as beautiful as roses are, they are attacked by a number of very stubborn diseases. So much so that there are some harassed gardeners who have given up growing them, because of the amount of time that has to be spent in keeping them healthy. Happily, however, most people love roses to such an extent that they are prepared to make some effort to preserve their beauty, but everybody hopes that the day will come when they will be free from these scourges. Actually much work is being done in research stations in various countries to discover new chemicals and to breed disease-resistant strains, but most of this work has not advanced far enough yet to be of any great practical value to ordinary rosarians. For those readers who are interested in this 'back room' activity, an account of some of the progress that has been made over more recent years is given later in this chapter.

Broadly speaking, there are three main types of diseases that affect roses. These are those brought about by the action of (1) fungi, (2) bacteria and (3) viruses. Of these the first category is by far the most serious. Both fungi and bacteria lack chlorophyll and are thus unable to synthesise starch in the same way as plants. In consequence they sponge on higher forms of plant life in order to live. Some of the fungi, *parasites*, attack healthy plant tissues, while others, known as *saprophytes*, live on dying or decaying vegetable matter. The virus diseases are due to minute bodies, that are capable of multiplying, which exist within the plant cells. They are so small in size that they cannot be detected through an ordinary microscope, but need an electron microscope to be seen. Although the present state of our knowledge suggests that there are about eight viruses that attack roses, they have not yet become a serious menace in this country.

In order that readers can recognise the various diseases that are likely to attack their roses, the nature, symptoms and methods of their control are discussed in the ensuing paragraphs.

Mildew

This disease, which is found on roses wherever they grow throughout the world, is due to a fungus, *Sphaerotheca pannosa*, which is exclusive to members of the rose family. In some years it appears to attack more severely than it does in others. Contrary to common belief, it is not more prevalent in wet weather than when it is dry. In fact, because one of the causes of bad infestations is the drying out of the roots, there is a marked tendency for the disease to be more serious during a hot dry summer than in a cold wet one. Excessive moisture, however, does encourage its development when its spores alight on the leaves particularly when other conditions, such as temperature, are right, but it is doubtful whether this applies to any greater extent to mildew than to any other fungus. It is for this reason that it is always a wise precaution to avoid wetting the rose foliage when watering. Roses that are planted in very sheltered positions, or that are climbing a wall, tend to be affected by mildew more than those that are in good open sunny positions. This is probably due to the fact that a good air circulation helps to keep the leaves dry.

The symptoms of mildew are so familiar to experienced gardeners that it is almost unnecessary for any description to be given, but for the benefit of beginners, the main ones are described. Mildew attacks roses at almost any time in the season. At the outset the leaves have a slightly reddened and twisted appearance, which usually sounds the alarm to the expert. This is soon followed by the arrival of white or greyish-white spots on the young leaves and stems. These soon spread and all the affected leaves, stems and seed pods become covered in white. In severe attacks, the plants look as if they have been dusted with talcum powder. As the fungus gets a hold, minute suckers or *haustoria* penetrate the skin of the leaves and absorb the nourishment stored in them. Their cells die and the dead tissues, which become black, give the appearance of black spot.

With established roses, there are three main steps that can be taken to minimise the effect of mildew:—

(1) In autumn, collect all the fallen leaves and cut away any stems that have been affected and burn them immediately. As the spores of this fungus winter over on them, this prevents the disease flaring up in the spring.

(2) When the trees are dormant they should be sprayed with Bordeaux Mixture (See page 145). This might be followed by

spraying again, using Karathane (dinocap), this time, after pruning.

(3) To destroy the summer spores as they are produced, the bushes should be sprayed with Karathane at intervals of ten days. On no account must Bordeaux Mixture be used on rose trees when they are in leaf, otherwise the leaves will be disfigured.

There is, however, one fortunate feature of mildew that has been known for a long time. This is that the susceptibility of different roses varies considerably. In consequence, a gardener, who is making a new rose garden, can by careful selection have roses that are completely immune. This is one of the factors that should always be taken into account when buying roses. It will be appreciated that conditions vary from one garden to another so that it is difficult to say with absolute certainty that any particular variety will always be immune, but experience has shown that the following selection of hybrid teas can be backed to have a good chance of being fairly satisfactory in this respect:—

Blue Moon	Gavotte	Princess
Brandenburg	Golden Melody	Rose Gaujard
Chicago Peace	Grandpa Dickson	Royal Highness
Colour Wonder	John S. Armstrong	Shannon
Diorama	Peace	Silver Lining
Dorothy Peach	Perfecta	Super Star
Fragrant Cloud	Pink Favourite	Wendy Cussons

Black Spot

This disease is caused by a fungus, *Diplocarpon rosae* Wolf. Unlike mildew, there is a tendency for attacks of black spot to be more severe during spells of wet weather. Its incidence is also greater in cold damp places. Although it can appear at almost any time in the season, sometimes as early as May, black spot does not usually show itself until the beginning of August. Anytime after this date, it can appear suddenly and within a very short time the bushes can become defoliated particularly at their lower extremities, where the disease invariably sets in. Up-to-date research work has established that this increased activity of the disease later in the season is due to the plants becoming more susceptible to attack and not to an increase in the virility of the fungus.

The first symptoms of the disease are the appearance of black or dark brown spots on the leaves, which gradually increase in size and eventually join up, forming a large black area. Soon the remaining parts of the leaves turn yellow and they fall off, leaving the trees ultimately completely bare. The spores are airborne, or they are splashed up by the rain from the ground on to the lower leaves. Under favourable conditions, the fungus grows on the leaves and penetrates beneath the skin of the leaves and steals the plant's vital supplies of food. As a result the characteristic black spots appear on them. These are actually dead tissues that have degenerated through lack of food. Ultimately when the leaves are falling off, there is a serious loss of vitality.

So far no means has been devised to eradicate black spot after it has attacked a plant. The steps that are taken against it are therefore aimed at preventing it settling in and controlling its subsequent spread. It is a well known fact that the incidence of black spot is very low in the smoke-laden atmosphere of industrial areas. This is presumably because the chemicals in the air maintain continuously a preventive layer on the surface of the leaves. Thus, the present methods of control have the same objective. Unfortunately, however, under clear air conditions, rain inevitably washes off the protective layer applied. So at the present it is necessary to spray the bushes with a fungicide at intervals of no greater than two weeks and to be prepared also to repeat the treatment after rain at any time during this interval, if complete protection is to be sustained. There are a number of proprietary preparations on the market in this country that are effective when used for controlling black spot. These variously contain the fungicides Captan (Orthocide), Phaltan (Folpet), Maneb and Dichlofluanid (Elvaron). There is also one preparation being sold, that is a mixture of Phaltan and Karathane and thus simultaneously affords protection against both black spot and mildew.

It has been long advocated that all the fallen leaves should be collected and burnt. It has now been established that this fungus does not winter over on the leaves on the ground, but on those still on the trees and stems. Thus, strictly speaking, there is no necessity to gather up the fallen leaves, but there is none other than cold comfort in this thought because other equally dangerous fungi, such as mildew and rust, do survive the winter on the fallen leaves. It is therefore advisable to gather up as far as possible all the infected leaves on the ground during the autumn months and burn them.

Any leaves and stems attacked by black spot, still remaining on the tree should be cut off at this time and also burnt.

Over more recent years many rosarians have become depressed by the prevalence of black spot. There is indeed some evidence that it is becoming more wide-spread and is appearing on roses in urban districts, where it had not been seen previously. This probably is a direct result of the introduction of the Clean Air Act, which has restricted the amount of sulphur-laden smoke, that is emitted into the atmosphere. Rose growers can, however, get some consolation from the latest recommendations of the Royal National Rose Society (see *Rose Annual* 1969). In the past, they have had considerable trouble with black spot in their display gardens at St Albans, but during the summer of 1968 only three varieties were affected following the use of their newly devised spraying programme. This consists of spraying roses with Bordeaux Mixture (8 oz to 2½ gallons of water), at the rate of 1 gallon to 7–10 square yards, immediately following the shortening of the bushes at the end of November to minimise the ill-effects of strong winds. When carrying this out a coarse nozzle should be fitted to the sprayer, otherwise it is likely to become clogged. The Royal National Rose Society then spray with Maneb, commencing about mid-June. It is particularly emphasised that this should be carried out regularly during August and September, when the onslaught of the fungus is always so severe. It is also strongly recommended that all new roses bought should be either sprayed with or dipped in Bordeaux Mixture on receipt from the nurseryman.

It would be very comforting if it were possible to give a selection of roses that are likely to be immune from black spot, just as was done in the case of mildew. Alas! this is impossible. The sad truth is that United States research workers have shown conclusively that not only are there more than 50 different races of this fungus, but also that no varieties of garden roses are known to be immune from this devastating disease.

Rust

Rust disease, which is caused by a fungus called *Phragmidium mucronatum*, is very troublesome in the districts in which it strikes. It is so serious that infected plants, if left unaided, will often die in the first year of infection. All the evidence available suggests that no garden roses are immune from it and the hardy hybrid varieties are particularly susceptible. It has, however, the pecularity that it only occurs in certain districts in the United Kingdom, although there is at the present time some evidence of it spreading further afield. It is particularly prevalent in the south-west of England and Northern Ireland, while the north of England and Scotland are comparatively free. Another characteristic is that the winter spores need to be exposed to frost in order that they can come to life again in the spring.

The first signs of the disease appear in April, when spore-containing rust-coloured pistules, like swellings, appear on the undersides of the leaves. These are followed by orange-coloured spores in June. This is a particularly dangerous period in the life cycle of the fungus because at this time the spores germinate very freely and widespread infection occurs. A little later in August, there is another change in colour, this time from bright orange to black. In this form, the fungus is carried over the winter, only to recommence its activity in the following spring.

Years ago, rust was considered to be incurable and when it appeared it was the practice to dig up the infected rose trees and burn them, but nowadays, with current techniques and newer fungicides, it is possible to obtain control of the disease within a year. There are three stages in the course of action that is recommended:—

(1) In spring, if any signs of the disease appear, any infested leaves and stems should be cut away, collected in a paper bag and immediately put on the bonfire.

(2) During the summer, if the disease persists or appears, the roses should be regularly sprayed with a recommended proprietary specific, that usually contains Maneb, Zineb, Thiram or Manozeb, combined with Karathane.

(3) The autumn following an attack is a very important period. At this time, all fallen leaves that can possibly be collected should be removed from the beds and burnt. The few remaining leaves should be dug in under the surface of the soil in order to minimise the action of frost. Any infected stems should be also cut away and destroyed. If the beds have been well-mulched and the space is available the layer of humus should be carefully raked off and buried about 12 inches below the surface of the ground in a part of the garden where roses are not grown. Since the spores do not winter over unless they are frozen, a good covering of straw, shredded

polythene or other clean insulating material is well worth putting on the beds. Lastly, the rose trees should be sprayed with Bordeaux Mixture at the rate given for black spot (See page 145).

Other Fungus Diseases

There are a number of other fungi that attack roses, but none are so prevalent as the three already described, but several of them are worth mentioning because a gardener might at anytime meet one of them in his garden.

Leaf Scorch (*Septoria Rosae*. Desm.) Although it is rather uncommon and there is fortunately some scientific evidence that suggests that it does not affect hybrid roses, this could be a serious disease because roses that are exposed to it in two successive summers rarely survive. Affected roses commence by having minute yellowish-green patches, scattered over the surface of the leaves, that become yellowish and increase in size, gradually change to brown and become bordered with a dark reddish or purplish line as time passes. On young leaves, these brown areas fall out, leaving what look like 'shot holes'.

All diseased leaves, both on the ground or on the trees, should be collected and burnt. In the spring, following an attack in the previous summer, the young leaves should be sprayed with a copper-based fungicide.

Anthracnose. This disease is due to a fungus *Sphaceloma rosarum*. It is not entirely unknown in this country. It first manifests itself on the leaves as paler green spots, that become in time dark brown and afterwards purplish black, often with a dull brown or purplish rim. As with leaf scorch, the tissue of these spots ultimately falls out and a 'shot hole' effect is given to the leaves. The disease also attacks the stems and hips.

All the affected parts should be removed and burnt and the rose trees sprayed with a copper-based fungicide. All infected leaves and stems on the ground should be collected and also burnt.

Die-back. True Die-back is a fungus disease, which is caused by a fungus, *Gnomonia rubi*. Rambler roses are particularly prone to attack by this disease. It causes serious dying off of the wood.

On the other hand, roses of all types suffer from time to time from the dying back of their shoots. There are a number of causes for this happening. Among the most common are frost, lack of water, resulting in drying out, damage to the tissues by careless pruning, the snapping of the shoots by strong winds or rough handling, etc.

Such damage is often wrongfully termed 'die-back'. Although such damaged wood in the first instance is not diseased, it is liable, however, to become an excellent growth medium for fungi. All such dead parts must therefore be cut back to a healthy bud, even as far as the union, if necessary. If this is not done, the dead tissues are likely to spread eventually into the roots, when the plant would die. The most common fungus diseases that attack dead shoots are the various cankers, of which stem canker is extremely common and the most destructive.

Stem Canker. This is caused by the fungus, *Leptosphaeria coniothyrium.* As stated above, this infection occurs at wounds, and also at dormant buds on shoots, frequently at the cut end after pruning. The initial signs are yellowish or reddish, spotted and streaked, pimply or water saturated areas that soon become brown. The affected parts continuously grow in size and eventually they extend round the full girth of the stalks for several inches. As the fungus develops minute black spots appear.

Cutting back all the dead wood, irrespective of whether it is diseased or not, as soon as it is seen, to where the growth is healthy and burning all such cuttings, is the only measure that can be taken to prevent the spread of this disease.

Griphosphaeria corticola. This is another fungus disease, which is fairly common in this country. It shows its presence by dead patches on the stems. Once again, the only remedy is to cut away all the diseased wood and burn.

Diseases Due to Bacterial Action

There are a number of diseases that attack plants that are caused by bacterial action. The most prevalent of these among roses is Crown Gall.

Crown Gall. This disease manifests itself by the appearance of swellings, usually low down on the rose tree, often at the shank of the understock. It is caused by the bacteria, *Agrobacterium tumefaciens,* which brings about an abnormally high rate of cell division. Galls do, however, sometimes appear on any of the stems and even on the roots. The only cure at present is to cut away the gall and paint the wound with Stockholm tar to prevent re-infection and infestation by fungi.

More recent research, however, suggests that these galls have no deleterious effect on the health of their host. It has also been discovered that where roses are planted in raised beds, that have good aeration and drainage, crown gall rarely occurs. During the past two or three years a chemical, Bactinin, has been found to be effective, when painted on active galls that develop on the stem of apples, peaches and apricots. This chemical is now being tested on roses.

Deficiency Ailments

Chlorosis. Already the effects of the lack of certain essential elements in the soil on roses has been mentioned (See Chapter 8). As is known, one of the possible ailments is chlorosis, which is caused by the absence of iron and manganese. The effect of this shortage often shows in plants growing in alkaline soils or in ones that have been overfed with phosphate, because under such conditions these two important foods become tied up in chemical forms that cannot be absorbed by plants. No additions of iron and manganese made in the ordinary way, can remedy this defect because they are immediately trapped. Fortunately, however, this difficulty can be overcome by supplying chelating agents, containing these essential elements to the soil. They are available in this form in a product called Sequestrene-Plus, which contains chelates of iron and manganese, together with active magnesium. It is applied to the soil, preferably in spring as a suspension in water, prepared according to the maker's instructions.

The symptoms of chlorosis, which usually appear in late spring, are yellowing of the leaves and stems. The leaves ultimately shrivel and fall off. The plants become weedy and stunted in growth. It should, however, be borne in mind that deficiency of other elements, such as nitrogen, will cause yellowing of the leaves and feeble growth. As Sequestrene-Plus is an expensive chemical, it is as well to check that chlorosis is the true cause of the condition before embarking on this treatment.

Future Methods of Combating Rose Diseases

Considerable work is being carried out in various parts of the world, with the view to eradicating diseases, particularly the more serious ones, such as mildew, black spot and rust. There are a number of different approaches to this subject that are being made. Firstly, there is research work being carried out on the development of new fungicides that are specifics against the different fungi. Particular attention is being paid in this sphere to the development of systemic compounds similar in their action to those that are now so successfully being used by agriculturists and horticulturists in the destruction of crop pests. Secondly, serious attempts are being made to breed disease-resistant cultivars. Thirdly, very important studies are being made, particularly in this country, of the biochemical, physical and physiological changes that take place in the metabolism of roses, both when healthy and when stricken by various fungus diseases and bacteria. The latter is inevitably a slow task, but one that will ultimately make tremendous contributions to our knowledge of this subject. Mainly because the work is rather more advanced in them than it is in the last-named approach, the first two are considered in a little more detail in the next few paragraphs. They are of necessity only dealt with briefly, but it is hoped that the accounts will suffice to give the readers the impression that some good progress is being made and to emphasise the enormity of the tasks that scientists are undertaking.

Recent Developments in Fungicides

More materials are being developed in the United States that are able to control mildew after it has become established. Several of these are proving so good that tests show treated roses to be quite free of the disease, while it thrives on others, that have not been sprayed, in the same bed only a few feet away.

It is, of course, in the field of systemic fungicides that progress is most desirable because of their labour-saving qualities and of their ability to withstand rain. Even in this field, there is some hope of success, because there is under trial at the present time a compound, called Benlate (a 50% wettable formulation of the methyl ester of 1 - (butylcarbamoyl) - 2 - benzimidazole carbamic acid, which is expected to be on the retail garden market in the course of the next year or two. It is claimed to have systemic qualities when used as a fungicide against a number of fungus parasites, including mildew and black spot. There are in addition several other chemicals that give systemic protection. These are substances showing much promise, but, which probably require further development before they can be marketed.

Breeding of Disease-resistant Cultivars

Since the end of the Second World War, there has been considerable pressure put on rose hybridists to breed disease-resistant roses. This is, of course, no easy task, but despite this, quite a lot of progress has been made. Even so, it will be quite a long time before such roses are likely to be commercial propositions.

During the past few years considerable work, having this object in view, has been carried out on black spot at the Beltsville Research Station of the Crop Research Division, Agricultural Research Service, U.S. Department of Agriculture. A considerable amount of time had at first to be devoted to obtaining information regarding the nature of the fungus itself, its physiological effect on roses, when it attacks them, and any changes in the metabolism that takes place in the plants when they are infested with it during the growing season. Two of the earliest problems that had to be solved in this research programme were how to rear strains of the black spot fungus that could be reproduced over long periods of time in the laboratory and how to devise methods of comparing their effect on various species and cultivars of roses. Although there is still a long way to go before the ultimate goal of breeding disease-immune roses can be attained, some very useful information has already been obtained. Among it, is the following:—

(1) There are more than fifty different races of black spot. So if one fails to get a hold on anybody's roses, there is a good chance that one of the remaining would do so.

(2) Definite confirmation has been secured that no matter how diligently spraying is carried out earlier in the season, black spot always attacks more severely in August and September. This research work indicates that this is not because the fungus becomes more virile, but because the plants are more susceptible later in the summer owing to changes in the metabolism of the plants.

(3) Almost every garden rose known today is susceptible to attack by black spot. Thus, the chances of producing disease-resistant roses by inter-breeding these types is very small.

(4) Some of the species roses, particularly, *Rosa multiflora* Thunb., *R. pisocarpa* Gray, *R. rugosa* Thunb., R × alba L., *R. woodsii* Lindl., *R. soulieana* Crep., resist attacks of many, if not all, of the races of black spot fungus to which they are exposed.

The fourth finding suggested that crossing garden roses with species roses might result in black spot-resistant roses. Unfortunately it did not prove so easy as all that. This is because species roses have diploid tissue and our present garden roses have tetraploid (See page 210). Unions between roses with these two different types of cells invariably result in seedlings that are sterile. In consequence, the only hope of rearing roses fairly quickly from such parents is to convert the diploid tissue of the species roses into tetraploid and then cross them with garden roses.

This, in fact, has now been done in America. It has been known for some time that it was possible to change the diploid tissues of commercially important species, such as cranberries, blueberries, peaches, apples, chestnuts and grapes, by treating their leaf buds with an alkaloid, colchicine, which is extracted from the corms of the autumn crocus. Applying the same process to species roses, scientists at Beltsville have now succeeded in producing tissues of species that have tetraploid characteristics. From this point, it is hoped that there will arise a new race of garden roses that will be black spot resistant, or even immune. We must, however, all be very patient because given a straightforward run, this could take another ten years to reach fulfilment!

CHAPTER FOURTEEN

Modern Climbing Roses

In Chapter 4, the use of modern climbing roses in present-day gardens has already been dealt with at some length. There is little doubt that, but for the introduction of this type of rose, climbers would have largely disappeared long ago because so many of those of former days grew so vigorously and to such great heights that small gardens would not be able to accommodate them. In addition, the old fashioned ramblers had the very serious fault of only flowering for a short period, in some cases as little as three weeks. This is a characteristic that is untenable under modern conditions. The newer climbers, irrespective of whether they are ramblers or large flowering climbers, grow quite modestly – very few exceed 10 feet in height. One of them in particular, Aloha, is rarely taller than 6 feet, and is an excellent subject for any wall or boundary fence of a confined space. All of them are recurrent in flowering. Between all the varieties, they produce very lovely blooms, ranging in form from single flowers, many of which are very colourful replicas of those of floribunda and species roses to full size well-formed hybrid tea-shaped flowers, growing singly or in clusters. All of them are superb for modern gardens, and are so very versatile as well, that a cultivar can be found for almost any purpose.

The interesting thing about these modern climbing roses is that a large proportion of them fall into two categories. The members of one group have been derived from the repeat-flowering rambler, New Dawn, and those of the second have arisen from an entirely new species rose discovered by Wilhelm Kordes. Perhaps what is very remarkable about them is that they both came by accident some years before post-war conditions made it so essential to have modest-growing, repeat-flowering climbing roses in the garden.

The first change came about in 1930, when the very vigorous rambler, Dr W. Van Fleet, threw a sport, New Dawn. This rose is almost identical with its parent as far as the colour of its flowers is concerned – they are both a rather charming delicate pale flesh pink. Both have blooms that are medium sized and full in petallage. There are, however, two very important differences. New Dawn is far less vigorous in its growth and does not spread itself like its fore-bear, only reaching 8 feet in height. As it is a rambler, it still needs to be pruned after it has completed its flowering, but it never gets into a tangled mess like the old time varieties. Just a little cutting back and tying in is usually sufficient to keep it under control and this can be delayed until the winter. The other very important quality, that it possesses, which its parent has not, is recurrent flowering. Both these characteristics have indeed made New Dawn and its many progeny much sought-after for use in present-day gardens. Naturally hybridists, visualising the great possibility of a race of climbing roses with these much desired attributes, soon got busy breeding, making this new rose one of the parents. Everything went to plan. Many roses, even some of the latest of our climbers, can claim to have this remarkable rose, either as a parent, or in their pedigree. Perhaps among the loveliest of its progeny are pink Bantry Bay, Blossomtime, with its lovely blooms in two-tone pink, Coral Dawn, which has pink flowers, velvety dark-red Don Juan, carmine-crimson Parade and orange-apricot Schoolgirl.

Late in 1940, when the nations of the world were busily engaged in war, another chance happening occurred. This one was also destined to have a profound influence on modern gardening. For many years the famous German rose breeder, Wilhelm Kordes, had been striving to breed strong, healthy, remontant roses, that could stand up to the low winter temperatures that existed in the more northerly parts of Europe. With this object in view, his attention was attracted to the species, *Rosa rugosa*, which could stand temperatures well below freezing point and which was one of the few roses found in nature that had the desired quality of recurrent flowering. Un-fortunately, all past attempts to cross this species with garden roses, so as to combine the hardiness of *R. rugosa* and the large, many petalled flowers of the latter had failed. Every time seedlings had been obtained, they were sterile; so further breeding was not possible. The reason for this handicap is the same as that discussed in Chapter 13 in connection with the crossing of species roses with hybrid tea roses to obtain disease-resistant hybrids. This is that the cell tissue of *R. rugosa* is diploid in type, while that of garden roses is tetraploid, and the union of such roses always produces progeny with triploid tissues. Such roses are almost always infertile. On very rare occasions a seedling turns up as the result of such crossings, that is fertile. This was exactly what Kordes experienced in 1940. He discovered a rose from the self-pollination of *R. rugosa* × *R. wichuraiana* Max Graf, which, in addition to having the qualities that he was seeking, was fertile. This rose is now known as *R. kordesii* and is, in fact, the head of a new species. This new rose has now produced in little under 30 years a series of very beautiful roses, that are all modest growers, mostly not exceeding 10 feet in height, and that bloom repeatedly, producing large full petalled flowers. Certainly they are the very roses that present small garden owners require. Although a selection of such roses have already been listed in Chapter 4, they are so beautiful and so valuable for use in modern gardening that it is worthwhile mentioning some of them again. Since 1954 more than 20 *kordesii* climbers have been created. Unfortunately not all of them are obtainable in this country, which is certainly a great loss to British gardeners, because the beauty of the missing ones is so very much appreciated in Germany and elsewhere. Of those on the market here, particular mention is made of scarlet Alexander von Humboldt, Dortmund, with its crimson flowers each with a white eye, crimson Hamburger Phoenix, Köln am Rhein, which has somewhat formless, large full, deep pink blooms, pale yellow-coloured Leverkusen, which is continuous or recurrent in flowering throughout the summer and autumn, blood red, semi-double Parkdirektor Riggers, deep rose-pink Ritter von Barmstede, which, left untrained, will sprawl vigorously over the ground and gives excellent ground cover and Zweibrucken, which has deep crimson flowers.

Perhaps inspired by the development of these two very attractive types of climbers, in their wake there has come, in addition, over the same years from rose breeders, a wide variety of new modest-growing remontant climbing roses with a rather different ancestry. Of these, six, at least, deserve particular mention. They are scarlet Copenhagen, Danse du Feu, which has the most vivid orange scarlet flowers, Golden Showers, which can be used both as a specimen shrub or a climber, semi-double, deep yellow High Noon, Royal Gold, which grows the loveliest large deep yellow hybrid tea-type flowers, either singly or in clusters, the darkest scarlet Guinée, which was first introduced in 1938, and the scarlet crimson, single-flowered pillar rose, that is so appropriately named Soldier Boy.

With so many modest growing climbers to choose from, there is indeed no reason why this type of rose should be absent from any garden, no matter how small it may be.

CHAPTER FIFTEEN

Miniature Roses

Already in Chapter 3, the great value of miniature roses in layout plans has been discussed and a selection of bush varieties has been given. This type of rose is so fascinating and lovely that it is of value to spend a little more time learning more about it. These roses are so appropriate to small gardens, paved courtyards, the limited space of a flat balcony or, even, a window box, it is surprising that they do not enjoy in this country the great degree of popularity, that they have in the United States. As is known, many of them produce blooms that are exact replicas of their larger relatives, with the same wide range of vivid colours, that is associated with the hybrid tea and floribunda roses. The bush varieties never exceed 15 inches in height, only a small number are actually as high as this, some are short as 5 inches, which gives tremendous scope when roses are required to be utilised on a small scale. What makes them still more attractive is that some varieties can now be obtained as standards and climbers, so it is possible to make use of miniatures in order to create complete small rose garden layouts.

Miniature roses are by no means a new innovation. They have been known for at least 160 years. The first was brought to this country in 1810 from Mauritius. At this time, this tiny rose was named *Rosa lawrenceana* in honour of a very famous flower painter Miss Lawrence, who published a book of rose paintings in 1799. An illustration in the *Botanical Magazine* shows it to be a single rose, with slender, very pointed petals, growing separately from one another, which are blush white, tipped with rose, in colour. This picture also shows its leaflets to be similar to those of the more miniature varieties that are grown today. Although this rose reached these shores from Mauritius in 1810, there is considerable evidence to show that it did not originate there. There is little doubt that it was translated to this island from the Far East by an early traveller. It has in fact the characteristic of the China Rose of producing flowering shoots one after the other in rapid succession from each of the leaf axils all along its stems. In consequence, this new rose was ultimately renamed *R. chinensis var. minima.* There are some authorities who consider that this rose had been dwarfed at some time by the Chinese or Japanese, in much the same manner as they create their bonsai trees.

The next step in the development of this race of roses was the appearance of *Rosa roulettii* a few years later, but there is some mystery, even today, regarding how it came into being. A Dr Roulette, claimed to have discovered it in Switzerland and gave it his name. It was thought for some time to be identical with another small-growing rose 'Pompon de Paris', but there are some experts who assert that the latter differs from it by being both taller and more bushy. Despite, however, the controversy, that has raged for many years on the question of the authenticity of the origin of *R. roulettii*, it has played a very important part in the development of these very beautiful dwarfs and is undoubtedly the forerunner of the midget roses that are so well-known in these days and that are so appropriate to modern small gardens.

One of the first seedlings of *R. roulettii* was white-eyed, deep crimson Peon, which is also known as Tom Thumb, which is even more dwarf than its parent. This was raised in 1935 by the Dutch rose grower, de Wink, who with his fellow hybridist, Pedro Dot, in Spain, was destined to play an outstanding role in the building of this new category of roses. During the Second World War, and for a few years afterwards, there appears to have been a continued rivalry between these two men. During this period, a succession of new varieties was introduced, first by the Dutchman, and, then, by the Spaniard. Among these were rose-red Midget and white, shaded faint pink, Pixie (also known as Little Princess) by de Wink in 1940, Dot's carmine-red Baby Crimson (Perla de Alcanada) in 1944, followed one year later by Perla de Monserrat, which has clear pink blooms. In 1946, de Wink introduced lilac pink Sweet Fairy, which is a seedling of Peon. Dot replied in 1947 by raising the very tiny crimson Mon Petit, possibly the smallest of all, being only 5 inches high. Up to 1951 the range of colours that existed among miniature roses was restricted to pink to crimson, but in this year, Pedro Dot caused a revolution by breeding Rosina (also named Josephine Wheatcroft and Yellow Sweetheart), which is sunflower yellow in colour. After this, followed a series of yellow, coral pink, salmon, coral red, orange, scarlet and other vivid colours that completely established these lovely little roses for all times. Their success encouraged the creation of still more in other countries. In Germany, Kordes bred velvety-red Dwarf King (1957) and his compatriot, Tantau, Baby Masquerade,* which is an exact replica of its larger counterpart; and a French contribution came from Meilland with salmon, shaded coral, Cricri (1958), apricot shaded orange, Colibri (1959) and Scarlet Gem in 1961.

Over much the same period, a range of miniature roses was created by Moore in the United States. This includes ivory-white Easter Morning and coral pink Eleanor in 1960, Little Flirt, with its orange red flowers with reverse yellow and light red Diane in 1961 and, in 1962, salmon New Penny, that turns pink with age and light yellowish cream Yellow Doll.

There is nothing difficult about growing miniature roses. They like all the same soil and other conditions, that the bigger versions need for their well being. There is, however, one point regarding their cultivation on which a warning must be given. Because of their diminutive size, they are ideal for growing in rockeries, which they brighten up with their gay colours and cheerful appearance in the summer months when rock gardens can be rather dull. In many cases, particularly in true alpine gardens, the soil is on the poor and gritty side, and far from the best growing medium for roses. Pockets of rich loam containing well-rotted manure should therefore be made to accommodate miniatures if they are planted in such positions. It should also be remembered that, because the soil in a rockery is usually raised above the general ground level, they are extremely well-drained, even to the extent of being very dry. Similar conditions might also exist at the top of dry walls. In such circumstances, it is imperative to be sure that the miniatures are well-watered and that the ground is covered with a good layer of mulch during the summer months. As mentioned in Chapter 9, they require very little pruning. Those who wish to propagate miniature roses, should note that experts recommend that they should be grown from cuttings, otherwise the resulting cultivars lose their miniature form. If they are budded on to rootstock, they are coarsened and varieties, normally growing up to 8 inches high, will reach as much as 24 inches.

Earlier in this chapter reference was made to the fact that both standards of miniature roses and miniature climbers are now available. The standards which are very charming plants, usually have

* Classified by some rosarians as a dwarf floribunda.

stems of 12 to 18 inches high and perfectly shaped heads on a reduced scale. They are excellent for giving, for example, height to a bed of bush miniature roses or a sink garden planted out with them. Among the varieties that are grown as miniature standards are Baby Masquerade, Rosemarin and Scarlet Gem. In addition, bushes can be given a very beautiful background by planting behind them miniature climbers to match. For many years, there has been in existence Climbing Pompon de Paris, which unfortunately has only a very short flowering season, but while it does last, it affords a very lovely show of blooms. Among the other varieties now available are glowing rich coral rose Climbing Pink Cameo and Climbing Little Flirt, which never fails to thrill with its very charming semi-double flowers, that glow with their vivid colours of carmine-flame and rich gold at the base of their petals.

A Modern Climbing Rose 'Danny Boy' Deep Salmon Rose. Raised by
McGredy, 1969

A Miniature Rose. Rosemarin Soft Pink. Raised by Kordes, 1966

CHAPTER SIXTEEN

Perfume in Roses

The perfume of roses has already been discussed briefly in Chapter 4. It is now proposed to consider this very intriguing, but somewhat controversial subject, in greater detail. There is no doubt that fragrance is something that is expected by everybody in any rose. In fact, whenever a person is handed a rose, as often as not, the first thing, that is done, is to smell it. For a reason that is not easy to explain fully in the light of facts, many people associate with roses the strong, very lovely old rose perfume, that is characteristic of the ancient Damask Rose (*Rosa damascena*), and the Provence Rose (*Rosa centifolia*). So much so, that, because the proportion of modern roses in existence with this particular scent is relatively lower nowadays than it was in the past, it is often declared scathingly by some that present day roses have lost their scent! This is far from the truth. It is in fact very difficult to find a rose introduced in more recent times that is scentless. It is, however, admitted that the perfume, that they have, is not so often the traditional rose perfume, but something newer, more intriguing and often more subtle.

It is proposed to return later to the question of these rather more unusual, perhaps unexpected perfumes, that are possessed by so many of our present-day roses. In the meantime an attempt will be made to show that the 'rose' perfume of the Damask Rose was never the rule among members of the rose family even in former times. It was in fact much more the exception. If the pages of rose history are turned, it will be seen that these newer unusual scents found among our modern roses were often possessed by various species roses and their hybrids. In addition, some of them have scents that nobody would ever expect to find among roses. In fact, there are a few that are even different to anything known today.

Some of these very interesting perfumes that exist among various members of the rose family will now be examined. It is admitted that, in many instances, the particular species quoted are not always suitable for growing under present-day gardening conditions, but with the great complexity in the make up of today's roses, it may well be that they have had an influence at some point in the latter's development. They also serve to illustrate that there is nothing new about a rose not having the old-fashioned Damask Rose perfume and that the fact, that so many of our modern rose varieties of all types have not got it, does not mean that they have degenerated in any way. Looking first at roses that were flourishing in the gardens of our forebears from the beginning of the nineteenth century to the end of the first two or three decades of the present one, it might be a surprise to many to learn that two climbing roses, viz. Adélaide d'Orleans and which was first introduced in 1826 and Fécilité et Perpétue, born in 1827 and still flourishing in present-day gardens, both have a very distinct scent of primroses. This is a quality that is shared with the rose-pink lilac-coloured rose Spectablis (introduced in 1848), and it has been perpetuated in the twentieth century by the ramblers, Una and Débutante. Two other climbers have a strong scent of oranges. These are *Rosa polyanthus grandiflora* and the more recently introduced Wedding Day.

The smell of bananas is exuded by the species, *Rosa longicuspis*, which is a very lovely rose to grow up through the branches of a tree. Goldfinch and Francis E. Lester both have a very striking fragrance, which is reminiscent of a mixture of both oranges and bananas. Green apples is a common scent found among the older types of ramblers, particularly those that have been derived from the species *Rosa luciae*, instead of the more common *Rosa wichuraiana*. The well-known Albéric Barbier, which is still to be seen in gardens today, is a particularly good example of this type. Others are Alexandre Girault, François Juranville and the violet-coloured Veilchenblau. Raspberries are represented in the scent of the large flowering climber Cupid and Mme Gregoire Staechelin has that of sweet peas. These are but a few examples of the various scents that are possessed by members of the rose family, but they are sufficient to suggest that there is little reason for anybody to claim that the perfume of the damask rose is typical of roses. With this background it is indeed not surprising that so many of our modern roses with their very complex pedigrees do not possess it.

Turning now to hybrid tea and floribunda roses, there is one particular species that has undoubtedly played a very important part in the development of the perfumes that are found in our present day roses. This is *Rosa foetida*, that has itself a rather unpleasant odour such as its name suggests. It was a sport of this species, *Rosa foetida persiana*, that was used some 70 years ago by the French rose hybridist, Pernet Ducher, as a parent of the first non-fading yellow rose, Soleil d' Or, which became the forerunner of the wide range of vivid colours – yellow, orange, scarlet, bicolour and so on – that are so outstanding among the roses of today. From this time, it seems that the incidence of the old-fashioned rose perfume gradually diminished and these more unusual, often more delicate, ones rose into prominence.

It is, in fact, a very exhilarating experience to stroll around a rose garden as the sun is going down and the dew is beginning to rise, smelling each variety one by one. It is remarkable what a great variation in fragrance is to be found, even in the smallest garden. There is still in existence the traditional old rose scent of the Damask Rose being freely exuded by Crimson Glory, Eden Rose, Sutter's Gold and others, showing that it has not disappeared completely from the varieties that are currently grown. There are, however, numbers of others that are quite different; perhaps they seem strange for roses to some people. Mojave and Super Star, for example, are reminiscent of freshly gathered raspberries. The freshness of the woodlands is recalled by the violet scent of Dorothy Peach, Else Arnot and Hector Deane. One is reminded of apricots by the hybrid tea rose, Chantré, and Circus and Copper Delight from the ranks of the floribundas; lemons are brought to mind by the large flowering climber-cum-shrub rose, Golden Showers. Other floribunda roses have spicy scents, such as those of Elizabeth of Glamis and Iceberg, and the aromatics are represented by Border Coral. The memory of wild roses is stirred by Rumba and woodland violets by Radar. There are in fact many others, but these few examples, taken from the delightful and exciting range of fragrance that modern roses can offer, cannot fail to destroy the belief that roses have lost their scent. If there are still any doubters, they would become converted in no time, if they would make a point of smelling every rose that comes their way. It is amazing what an exhilarating experience it is when a new scent is unexpectedly discovered.

A SELECTION OF PERFUMED ROSES

HYBRID TEA ROSES		FLORIBUNDA ROSES	
Perfume	*Variety*	*Perfume*	*Variety*
Apricots	Chantré	Apricots	Circus
Fruity	Signora		Copper Delight
Old Rose	Charles Mallerin		Dearest
	Charm of Paris	Briar	Lilac Charm
	Chrysler Imperial	Cinnamon	Border Coral
	Crimson Glory		Columbine
	Duke of Windsor	Fruity	Alison Wheatcroft
	Josephine Bruce		Scented Air
	Milord	Old Rose	Arthur Bell
	My Choice		Magenta
	Papa Meilland		Orange Sensation
	Prima Ballerina		Overture
	Sterling Silver		Paddy McGredy
	Sutter's Gold		Woburn Abbey
	Wendy Cussons	Spicy	Elizabeth of Glamis
	Westminster		Golden Jewel
	Whisky Mac		Iceberg
Raspberry	Mojave		Jiminy Cricket
	Super Star	Tea-scented	Sea Pearl
Sweet (like			
face cream)	Silver Lining	Violets	Sweet Repose
Violets	Dorothy Peach		Radar
Violets	Elsa Arnot	Wild Rose	Rumba
	Honey Favourite		Violet Carson
	Hector Deane		

CHAPTER SEVENTEEN

The Quest for The 'Blue' Rose

During the past thirty years there have been many attempts to breed hybrid tea and floribunda roses with blue colour, but although some quite attractive roses, more particularly those with a lilac hue, have been produced, so far no 'true' blue roses have yet emerged. In fact, some of the very old roses, such as the gallica shrub, Cardinal de Richelieu (1840), the centifolia moss shrub, William Lobb (1855) and the hybrid tea-type rose, Reine des Violettes (1860) can claim to be nearer this objective than any that have resulted from any more recent planned programmes of hybridization. This comment applies equally to a number of others that were reared during the first three decades of the present century. These include the miniature rose, Baby Faurax (1924), the ramblers, Veilchenblau (1909), Rose Marie Viaud (1924), one of its seedlings, and Violette (1921).

Whether a true blue-coloured rose will ever be produced is still a matter of conjecture. There are some expert rosarians, who think that the possibilities are not very great. If this revolution does, however, come about, it might be either completely by accident or as the result of considerable research work, that reveals the mechanism by which this change can be brought about in the metabolism of the plants.

It is not of course within the scope of this book to study the chemistry of plant colours, but some readers might be interested in delving a little way into the more scientific aspects of this subject. It was thought some years ago by certain research workers that if a rose could be bred that contained a pigment called delphinidin, which is the pigment responsible for the colour of blue delphiniums, violet pansies and purple grapes, the goal would be reached. This conception was based on the knowledge that substances with similar chemical structures to that of delphinidin already existed in some roses. This hope, however, was soon dashed to the ground by the failure to detect the smallest trace of this chemical in any members of the rose family, that were examined. On the other hand, it is known that the same chemical, called cyanin, gives the red colour to red roses and the blue to cornflowers. The only difference in them is that it occurs in roses as a free phenol, whereas in the cornflower it is in the form of a potassium salt. At first sight to a chemist, it seems therefore to be a fairly simple task to change the condition in a rose so that the pigment is blue, but so far neither nature nor man has been successful in doing it. Moreover, it is known that the pH value of the cell sap has an influence on the colour of the pigment. When in an alkaline medium, it is blue, while in acidic, it is red. In fact, if a red rose is steeped in a weak solution of ammonia it will soon turn blue. This is an interesting experiment to make.

Other things are known about the cyanin. It changes from red to blue in the presence of the trace elements, magnesium and iron. Another factor that brings about the formation of floral colours is a process which is known as co-pigmentation, i.e. the mixing of various pigments. The present state of our knowledge is that the desired changes are capable of being brought about by what appear to be relatively simple chemical processes, but we have not yet been able to put them into operation within the plants themselves. The truth is that we know a great deal about the chemical constitution of plant pigments, which appear to be comparatively few in number, but we do not know what 'triggers off' the interactions between them. Thus, it seems that some time might yet pass before there is likely to be any approach made along these lines. It appears therefore that for the present time the only hope of producing truly blue roses lies in the continuation of the somewhat hit and miss tactics of the past.

Four different main strains of 'blue' roses are recognised at the present time. These are as under:—

(1) *The 'Grey Pearl' Strain.* For many years rose growers rejected seedlings that yielded lilac blooms as being unsuitable, but despite this it seems that some of the strain must have come through to Grey Pearl, which was introduced in 1945. It was fortunate that it did not meet the fate of all its predecessors because it has made an important contribution to the creation of 'blue' roses. In addition, it became the parent of Lavender Pinocchio, which has played an even greater role in this development. Among the progeny of Grey Pearl are: Lavender Pinocchio (1948), Lavender Garnette (1958), Heure Mauve (1962 – see Meilland Strain 1) and Intermezzo (1963).

(2) *The 'Lavender Pinocchio' Strain.* Among the roses derived from this rose are: Magenta (1955), Lavender Lady (1956), Lavender Princess (1960), Overture (1960 – See 'Meilland' Strain 1), Lilac Charm (1962), Pigmy Lavender (1961), Lavender Charm (1964), Lilac Dawn (1964), Lavendula (1965), Escapade (1967), Silver Charm (1968 – See 'Meilland' Strain 11), and Lake Como (1968 – See 'Meilland' Strain 11).

(3) *'Meilland Strain 1 (The 'Prelude' Strain).* The most important of these 'blue' roses are Pigalle (1951), Prelude (1954), Lavender Girl (1958), Violette Dot (1960), Overture (1960 – See 'Lavender Pinocchio' Strain) and Heure Mauve (1962 – See 'Grey Pearl' Strain).

(4) *'Meilland Strain 2 (The 'Peace' Strain).* The roses in this category have Peace in their pedigrees. A selection of them are Purpurine (1957), Sterling Silver (1957), Blue Diamond (1963), Blue Moon (1964), Silver Star (1966), Lake Como (1968 – see 'Lavender Pinocchio' Strain) and Silver Charm (1968 – see 'Lavender Pinocchio' Strain).

It will be noted that although the above are the main strains, already some crossing has taken place between them, e.g. Overture has ancestors from both the 'Lavender Pinocchio' Strain and the 'Meilland' Strain 1.

While it is not possible to go into this aspect in any great detail in these pages, it is of interest to observe that it has been found that the roses in all these four classes have some common characteristics. Perhaps the two most striking is that the rose, Charles P. Kilham, and the old species, *Rosa foetida persiana*, feature quite prominently in their pedigrees. Time has yet to show how these facts can lead rose hybridists to the creation of the much sought-after 'blue' rose. It will also prove whether, if it is produced, it will be an acceptable plant or whether it will just remain a collector's piece.

This is a fascinating subject and possibly one that some amateurs would like to pursue further. Those interested are recommended to read the paper given by Mr E. B. Le Grice to The Fourth International Rose Conference in London in July 1968 (See *The Rose Annual* 1969, pages 124–127). This gives an excellent analysis of the pedigrees of 'blue roses' and some useful references to books and papers on floral pigments.

There are in addition some other 'blue roses', the parentage of which are either unknown or which are 'strays'. These include Africa Star, Cologne Carnival, Godfrey Winn, Lavender Lassie (a shrub rose), Lilac Time, Mr Bluebird (a miniature), Song of Paris and Tristesse, (one of its parents is Charles P. Kilham).

CHAPTER EIGHTEEN

Exhibiting Roses

Quite often rose enthusiasts, encouraged by a visit to their local flower show, become interested in exhibiting roses. This is a very absorbing pastime. It calls for careful cultivation, continuous vigilance, patience and judgement to ensure that the exhibition blooms reach the show tent at the time of the peak of their perfection. During the last three or four weeks before the show very rigid control is needed, but showing roses is not too arduous a task for anybody who can spare the necessary time. The rewards in terms of satisfaction (but not cash!), gained by success are enormous. There is much fun to be had in showing and there is a great element of gambling in it that makes it particularly attractive to some people, who like a flutter. This is because, unlike other flowers, such as chrysanthemums, roses are only at the peak of their perfection for about two hours.

Classes of Entries at a Rose Show

Of course, local conditions up and down the country vary, but an appreciable number of horticultural societies have one thing in common in that they are affiliated to the Royal National Rose Society. In consequence, although there are some variations from place to place, the definitions and standards laid down by that body are the basis for showing in most provincial shows.

Obviously the first thing that a would-be exhibitor, irrespective of whether he proposes to show on the National or local scale, wants to know is what qualities a rose should have that is intended for exhibition. With a clear conception of this, cultivation and everything else can be directed towards this end. For these reasons, the requirements laid down by the Society for exhibiting at National Shows are given in detail below.

Type of Exhibition Classes

There are five principal ways in which roses are shown. These are:—

(1) Hybrid tea roses	Specimen blooms in boxes, without foliage
(2) Hybrid tea roses	Specimen blooms in vases, with own foliage
(3) Hybrid tea roses	Stems in bowls or vases, with own foliage
(4) Floribunda roses	Stems in bowls and vases, with own foliage
(5) Floral arrangements	Although this aspect is briefly touched upon in Chapter 20, it is not considered that this is a subject of this book

Hybrid Tea Roses in Boxes

In this case, the quality of the blooms is of paramount importance. No points are awarded for the good condition of the foliage and arrangement. They are exhibited in specially constructed boxes, which are fitted with tubes, that hold water and into which the roses are inserted. The boxes are usually made to hold 6, 12, 18 or 24 such tubes. The sizes of these boxes are strictly defined by the Society and are as under:—

All boxes must be 4 inches high in the front and 18 inches wide and of the following lengths:

Boxes to hold

24 blooms	3 ft – 6 inches
18 ,,	2 ft – 9 inches
12 ,,	2 ft – 0 inches
9 ,,	1 ft – 6 inches
6 ,,	1 ft – 0 inches

In all these boxes, the tubes must be 5 inches apart each way, measured from centre to centre of the tubes.

Hybrid Tea Roses – Specimen Blooms in Vases

Such exhibits consist of a specified number of blooms, not usually more than six. They are judged for the quality of the blooms and foliage, which must be the roses' own and attached to the stems, and points are also awarded for good arrangement.

Hybrid Tea Roses – Stems in Bowls and Vases (Formerly known as Decorative Roses)

In such entries, a specified number of stems of roses are arranged either in a bowl or a vase. The Royal National Rose Society has defined a stem as a flowering shoot with no lateral growths. For the purpose of the definition a lateral is a secondary growth arising from the flower stem bearing one or more latent eyes. It will thus be seen from this definition that the possibility of more than one bloom being borne on each stem is not precluded.

Generally speaking the size of blooms shown in this class is rather less than that in the case of specimen blooms, but their quality should be as good. Exhibits are assessed by the judges for quality of the blooms, arrangement, decorative beauty and/or form of blooms, or truss, and foliage.

Floribunda Roses – Stems in Bowls and Vases

Entries in this case are more or less the same in definition as the previous ones, except that, of course, to be of good standard, the cluster on each stem must be as large as is consistent with the variety being exhibited. Judging is done in exactly the same way as for stems of hybrid teas.

Finally, a rose grower, who intends to exhibit roses, needs to know exactly what the expressions 'hybrid tea roses' and 'floribunda roses' mean. These are very clearly described in the following quotations from the schedule of The Royal National Rose Society:

'The expression h.t. roses includes hybrid teas, hybrid perpetuals, teas and their like.'

'The expression floribunda roses embraces all hybrid polyantha, shrub and other roses (including floribunda – hybrid tea type), which are grown and staged in clusters, but not ramblers, poly. pompons or h.t. roses, classified as such in the Society's publication 'A Selected List of Varieties.'

WHAT IS A GOOD EXHIBITION ROSE?

Specimen Hybrid Tea Blooms

A good exhibition rose should be symmetrical in shape with the outside petals almost flat, the next row partly open; the inside petals should rise to a high point, forming a firm centre. Blooms with either split or 'scrambled' centres are regarded as poor blooms, which will only be awarded low points, if any at all. The rose should be true to colour and sparkling fresh. It should not be blemished by disease, insects or weather. There should be no damaged petals, which should also be clean, with no specks of dust or insects among them. In selecting roses for exhibition, special attention must be also given to the condition of the leaves, which should always be those of the selected roses themselves, growing on their stalks. They must be undamaged and be of a good healthy colour. It is an advantage to wash off any stains produced by fungicides with clean water. A green bud is not counted as a flower by the judges, and one that is just showing colour is regarded as a poor bloom, and is likely to be downpointed.

Floribunda Roses

A good entry in the floribunda rose classes is one that has the largest number of blooms in a cluster, consistent with the variety that is being exhibited. It should be remembered that different cultivars vary in the maximum quantity of flowers that they naturally produce on a cluster and a rose judge must take this into account when assessing any exhibit. Each bloom must be as fully out as possible and its stamens when visible, must still be golden and show no signs of blackening. A really good cluster will have a large proportion of flowers that are good and firm. The floribunda roses must have a fresh appearance and be true to colour.

Varieties of Roses Suitable for Exhibition Purposes

In former times, a number of roses that were excellent varieties for shows were not good garden roses. In these days, fortunately most of the good exhibition roses, if not quite so strictly controlled, can be used to give a good display of colour. To a limited extent, there are still some that are very excellent for bedding, but that have blooms that never quite reach the high standard called for on the show bench. It is important, therefore, particularly in the case of hybrid tea roses, for any gardener who wishes to show roses to be sure that he grows the right varieties. A small selection of both hybrid teas and floribundas that have featured in prize-winning exhibits at national shows over the past two or three years are given on page 180.

GROWING PRIZE-WINNING DOW ROSES

Cultivation

Given the care in planting and subsequently, that has been described in earlier pages, almost every rose, providing it is suitable for showing, will produce flowers that can be brought on for exhibiting. To achieve this objective, it is necessary to give them a little extra attention during the four weeks or so before the show date. At the beginning of this period the buds should be just showing colour. The leaves of the trees should then be sprayed with a specially blended rose foliar feed. This should be repeated every three or four days, always taking a great care to see that the coloured buds are not wetted, otherwise the outside petals might become disfigured. During the whole of the growing season the roses must be kept watered. This must be continued, but during the last month before the show, special care must be taken to avoid wetting the flowers. A strict vigil must be kept for the appearance of pests and diseases, and immediate steps must be taken to eradicate them in the event of any attacks. If this aspect of cultivation is neglected, the leaves are likely to be seriously impaired.

Pruning

The normal pruning processes, already described, are adequate for the production of exhibition quality flowers, except that it is helpful to limit the number of flowering shoots, to three or less on each tree, in order to encourage the growth of large blooms. Particularly in the case of the autumn shows, the dead flowers of the first flush of blooms should be removed so as to be sure that the next crop matures satisfactorily and in time.

Disbudding

This probably is the most important process in the growing of a large perfect specimen hybrid tea rose. When a variety produces three buds on a flowering shoot, the two side ones should be removed, providing the centre one is healthy and well-formed, so that the latter can develop to its fullest extent. Care should, however, be taken to see that they are broken or cut away cleanly, leaving no stumps. If such stumps still exist at the time of judging, the exhibit might lose points. Disbudding should be carried out as soon as the buds are large enough to handle. If forceps are used for the purpose, this can take place at a fairly early stage in the development.

In addition disbudding is a valuable means of controlling the time of blooming. If, for example, the centre bud is likely to be fully grown before the date of the show, it can be eliminated together with one of the side buds, leaving the other one to develop at a more appropriate time. Similar action can be taken when the centre bud is damaged or mis-shapened. As is known there are a number of varieties of hybrid tea roses (See page 36), that have a great propensity to produce their blooms in clusters. By selectively disbudding such plants, an exhibitor can take advantage of this quality when he has a succession of show dates to meet during the summer.

It will be appreciated from the definition of roses intended for entry into classes, where a number of stems, and not specimen blooms, is stipulated, that they are not necessarily disbudded.

Similarly no disbudding in the manner described above is done in the case of floribunda roses. All that is done is to remove early on the large centre bud of a cluster, which is always in advance of the others and some of the smaller ones in order to ensure that the maximum number of buds are fully open on the morning of the show.

Protection of the Blooms Against the Weather

At the outset it must be emphasised that one of the general regulations for exhibitions of The Royal National Rose Society, except the spring show, is that they must be 'grown in the open, using only individual bloom protectors'. If they are protected in any more elaborate way, they are regarded as having been produced indoors.

The normal practice is to cover each bloom individually as soon as the petals begin to unfurl with a conical bloom protector, clipped to a stake by means of a special fastener, which allows it to be adjusted up or down as required (See Fig. 21, page 175). These protectors are usually made of waxed paper, but it is possible to construct them out of moderately stiff polythene sheeting. The latter type has the advantage that the progress in the growth of the rose can be watched more easily, but it is very necessary to guard against water condensation, which is not so rapidly absorbed as in the case of the paper cones. Such protectors serve to give protection against rain and dew. Another precaution that is necessary with blooms, that are covered with a protector, is to be sure that they do not hit the cone in strong winds because of the damage that might be caused. Each of their stems therefore should be tied to a separate stake.

When the weather is very humid there is a great risk of condensation taking place inside a protector. In order that the bloom does

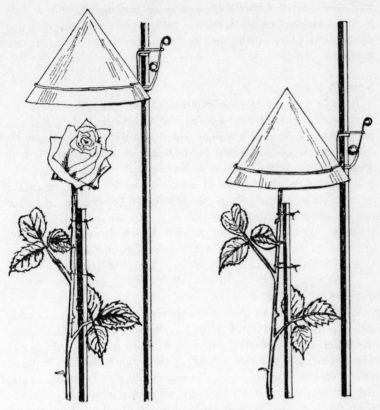

FIG. 21. *Exhibiting Roses – Weather Protection*

The blooms are protected with conical hoods against the effects of bad
weather. Each stem is loosely tied to a stake to prevent the flower coming
in contact with the protector in high winds

not become blemished, it is important always to raise the covers
under such circumstances. Another source of damage that might
occur to a bloom on a short stem, that is growing near the ground,
is mud splashed up by the rain. This can be prevented by placing
an inverted conical protector on the ground immediately below the
flower.

When buds are just showing a little colour, rain does not usually
do any damage to the petals, but if there is any fear of it doing so, it
is a good plan when a spell of rain is expected, to place polythene
sandwich bags, with the top corners cut away to give ventilation

over them and to secure them loosely at their mouths with a wire twist. Great care, however, must be taken to remove them when the danger has passed, otherwise condensation might be a greater menace.

Tying Blooms

It is the practice of some exhibitors to tie their blooms for the purpose of allowing them to develop within the tie and causing the petals to lengthen. This is done about two days before the show, using thick wool (preferably Berlin wool). A single strand is tied with a double twist round the widest part of the bud, omitting the two outer or guarding petals. It should not be tied tightly, so that it does not bruise or mark the petals. If it should become too tight after a day's growth, it should be loosened. The tie is usually kept in position until the flower is on the show bench. It should always be removed then, because the Royal National Rose Society's instruction to judges is to penalise any blooms that are still tied.

Cutting Roses for the Show

When roses are cut their stems should be immediately plunged into a bucket of cold water. When the required number is obtained, the lower leaves and thorns of each of them must be quickly cut away. This will facilitate arranging them when they are entered into a vase or bowl class. Each stem should also be split cleanly, using secateurs or a sharp knife, for a distance of about two inches from the bottom. This aids the absorption of water. They should then be steeped in a bucket of water.

When handling roses for exhibition, it must be borne in mind that sparkling freshness at the time of judging is an all-important factor. For this reason it has always been the practice to cut blooms in the cool of the evening previous to the show, or better still, if it is local, early in the morning of the day of the show. The increasing popularity of modern domestic refrigeration, however, has rightly or wrongly, tended to change this practice in more recent times. More and more roses are now often cut at the stage in their development that the exhibitor judges will allow them to mature on the morning of the show, if they are stored under cold conditions. The temperature of a refrigerator used, for this purpose, should be between 2° and 3°C. There is one danger that has to be guarded against in this practice and this is the risk of frost-bite. For this reason, it is an advantage to mount the container holding the roses with a wire frame of such size that a polythene bag can be put over it to cover the blooms. Some varieties are more subject to refrigerator burn than others. Which these are can only be ascertained by experiment. Red roses are particularly sensitive and will turn blue in an excessively cold atmosphere.

The exact point of time in its development that a rose must be out in order that it will be at its best when it is being judged is likely to vary from variety to variety. This must therefore be studied by the exhibitor at some time when a show is not imminent. Obviously the earlier it is picked the less it is open and the longer the time that it will need to reach maturity. When a rose is cut and stored in water at a low temperature, it will certainly develop at a much slower rate than it will do if left on the tree. With most varieties, this retardation causes them to produce rather larger blooms than they do if they are allowed to grow naturally.

Some exhibitors always add a chemical flower preservative to the water in which they keep their roses. There are others that are not so convinced that it does any good. In any case, it certainly does not do any harm.

Wiring Roses

At the shows of the Royal National Rose Society and its affiliated societies, it is legitimate to wire the necks of roses that are so weak that the blooms droop. This is a tricky business and an amateur is advised to practise doing it long before the show comes along. Otherwise some of his very best specimens are likely to be beheaded. The best way to do this is to take the seedpod between the first finger and the thumb of the left hand and with the right hand to hold a florist's wire of the correct length at a point $\frac{1}{2}$ to $\frac{3}{4}$ inch from its end. This end of the wire is then gently pushed into the seed receptacle, the wire is kept parallel to the stem and as close as possible to it. The wire is next firmly fixed by twisting it round the stalk at intervals of two inches, so that the wire and the stem become united. By bending the wire, it will then be possible to put the flower into any desired position without any risk of damage. It is as well to wire blooms at home before leaving for the show so that undivided attention can be given to this rather delicate operation. (Fig. 22.)

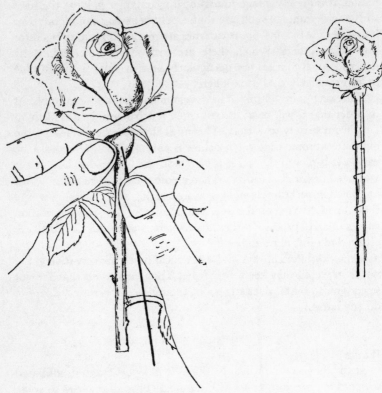

FIG. 22. *Exhibiting Roses – Wiring Blooms*

Inserting wire into the
receptacle. Great care
must be taken not to
break the flower off

A wired bloom

Packing Material for Vases

As has been pointed out already, good arrangement in the vase
classes earns points. This can only be done if the vases are suitably
packed. Almost any moderately hard cuttings from plants can be
used for this purpose, but experience has shown that reeds or
lonicera nitida are best. A good tip is to cut the packing into lengths
suitable for the size of the vases specified before leaving for the show.
If it is not possible to obtain supplies of the above mentioned,
stalks of privet, herbaceous plants, coarse grass, and, even, drinking
straws are excellent substitutes.

Transporting the Blooms to the Show

There is no doubt that by far the best way of transporting roses to the show is in containers of such a depth that the roses with the longest stems can be steeped in water. If a rose exhibitor has a car, it is worthwhile either making, or having made, metal containers of such a size that they will carry up to 20 blooms apiece. Each should be fitted with side handles and about two inches below the rim there should be soldered lugs inside the container. On the latter should be placed a wide mesh grill, which will help to keep the flowers apart. Further protection of the blooms can be afforded by covering each with tissue paper. To keep the containers steady during the journey to the show they should be placed in tailor-made crates, each holding not more than three.

For those who have only to travel a short distance to a show, or who have to use public transport, there are available nowadays excellent cardboard flower boxes with internal fitments, specially designed to prevent the blooms moving during transit. As these are usually non-returnable, many florists are only too pleased to give them away. If this method of packing is used, however, it is imperative to remember to put the roses into water immediately they are unpacked at the show.

Last Minute Preparations

Before leaving for the show a final check should be made to see that everything needed is taken. The list should include the show schedule, secateurs, scissors, a camel-hair brush, florist's wire, packing for the vases, name cards, if they are not supplied by the show organisers, wool for tying blooms, a pen, a small watering can, a duster, and, most important of all, spare blooms.

Staging the Blooms

On arriving at the show, a final assessment must be made of the blooms available and a decision made regarding how they should be best deployed among the various classes that have been entered.

Following this the flowers and foliage should be carefully examined to see that there are no insects or dust on the petals or dirt on the leaves. If necessary the petals should be cleaned by means of a camel-hair brush, while the leaves should be wiped with a damp soft cloth or tissue.

It is possible to manipulate or 'dress' the petals of the flowers to give them the appearance of being at the peak of their perfection, but this requires considerable skill. This is an art that should be learned from an experienced exhibitor. A warning, however, must be given that present-day judges frown on roses that have been over-dressed. It must therefore be done with discrimination. It should be remembered that some varieties are naturally so perfect, when fully developed, that, if they are touched, they will appear over-dressed. Isobel de Ortiz is a particular example of such a rose.

In staging, the roses must be well arranged in their containers, using adequate amounts of packing, because in the vase and bowl classes, this earns points. A would-be exhibitor must be a good showman. Everything must be done to impress the judge. Colours must be arranged so that they do not clash – a pink and a red, for example, should be separated by a white, cream or yellow rose. The blooms should be arranged as far as possible to form a triangle. In the case of a vase of three roses, one should be placed at the apex of a triangle and the other two at the extremities of its base; in the case of six, there should be three rows, the first at the top with one rose in it, the second lower down with two and there should be three roses in the bottom row. In the case of a box, the rows should be graduated in height by adjusting the level of the cups, from the highest at the back to the lowest in front. Whatever the class may be, the best blooms should always be positioned so that they catch the judge's eye and the more inferior ones should be placed in a less conspicuous situations. When putting the exhibit finally on the show bench, care should be taken to see that its colours do not clash with its neighbours. Finally, do not place it next to the entry, which is likely to be its greatest competitor. If it has more lowly companions, the judge will notice it more readily.

A SELECTION OF ROSES FOR EXHIBITION
Hybrid Tea Roses

Variety	Colour
Fragrant Cloud	Red (Geranium lake)
Montezuma	Deep salmon red
Red Devil	Scarlet
Super Star	Vermilion
Wendy Cussons	Cerise
Gavotte	Light pink and silver
Isobel de Ortiz	Deep pink and silver

Variety	*Colour*
Pink Favourite	Rose pink
Silver Lining	Pale rose and silver
Stella	Pink and cream
Memorium	White, tinted pale pink
Royal Highness	Blush White

Floribunda Roses

Anna Wheatcroft	Vermilion
Dorothy Wheatcroft	Bright red
Evelyn Fison	Vivid red with scarlet shading
Europeana	Deep crimson
Orange Sensation	Vermilion
Firecracker	Carmine with yellow at the base
Fred Loads	Vermilion-orange
Irish Mist	Orange-salmon
Dearest	Rosy salmon
Allgold	Golden yellow
Arthur Bell	Golden yellow
Iceberg	White

CHAPTER NINETEEN

Growing Roses in confined spaces — Patios, Terraces and Rockeries

Modern living has compelled many people during the past thirty years to dwell in town houses, small converted cottages and flats, where the space for gardening is only a paved patio, a terrace, a courtyard, often converted from a derelict backyard, or, possibly, a roof garden. Despite this, the love of gardens is so ingrained in many of them that there is still a great desire to grow flowers even under this handicap. As with gardeners, who have larger gardens, roses rank high among their preference for different plants. At first sight with the propensity of so many modern roses to grow so vigorous and tall, this might appear to be impossible. It can, however, be done by carefully selecting the varieties used.

The way in which roses are incorporated in the layout depends to a large extent upon the size of the garden concerned. If it is possible to make small beds in the paved area, then the cultural details are exactly the same as has been described already. The choice of types and varieties of roses must of course be restricted to the smaller and shorter-growing ones so that everything is kept in proportion to the size of space being planted out, the area is not completely dominated by them and there is still room left to grow, at least, some of the other interesting and lovely plants that make up a well-balanced garden. The use of half-standards and standards of the varieties of hybrid tea and floribunda roses desired is quite a good idea in a patio or terrace garden. The value of this type of rose is that they leave ample space in the beds, or containers, if they are used, below to plant out with other subjects and so increase the interest. In this respect, the possibilities of the more recently introduced standard miniature roses should not be overlooked.

While discussing this method of growing roses in a general way, attention must be drawn to the fact that this type of garden is often enclosed by high walls, particularly if it is situated in a built-up area. It is important therefore to make use of this vertical space to the fullest extent by growing climbing roses. Fortunately among the present-day climbers there are cultivars that have flowers that simulate the blooms of hybrid tea, floribunda and even the old-fashioned shrub roses. So there can be a great deal of variety among them, and it is, in fact, possible to have a complete rose garden growing up the walls. Perhaps for this purpose it is better to choose the shorter growing cultivars, a selection of which can be found on page 47. Mention, however, must be made of one particularly useful climber. This is Aloha, which has very full, pink, hybrid tea-type flowers with deeper reverse of petal. It grows to a height not exceeding 6 feet. Some gardeners find it to be a slow starter, but it is worth being patient with it, because it becomes very effective in time. Again, in urban districts, a courtyard might be in the shade for a considerable part of the day. In such a case, climbers like Danse du Feu, Gruss an Teplitz and Soldier Boy, which will grow quite successfully when planted on a north wall, should be chosen. Whatever roses are used, they should always be repeat flowering in character. In such a small space no other type can be possibly used, if a good and continuous display of colour is to be maintained.

Often it is not possible to make beds for roses in a paved area, either, because it is too small, or, the paving stones have been laid on a hard base, which would call for considerable work of excavation and the importation of good soil. In the heart of a town, the latter would certainly be a rare commodity and the disposal of the rubble that would be removed might be quite costly. Under such circumstances, therefore, the only way to grow roses is in containers. Fortunately they are so accommodating that this causes no difficulty, providing they are given just that little bit of extra attention that they need compared with when they are planted in the open ground. The author has two floribunda roses, Poulsen's Bedder, growing in pots, each 12 inches deep and with a diameter of approximately 18 inches, that have flourished over quite a number of years, producing a wealth of colour throughout each summer.

There is of course a wide range of pots and troughs, that can be acquired for this purpose. The actual choice of material and design depends largely on the environment in which they are to be placed. Whether it is, for example, contemporary or traditional. The question of expense also enters into the making of a decision. The most costly and, perhaps, more elegant are fashioned out of stone or lead, but more economical, but quite acceptable, replicas are available nowadays, made of cast stone and lead-coloured fibreglass. In some surroundings large terracotta-coloured clay containers, adorned with some decoration are equally as attractive, while white-painted wooden containers, made by a do-it-yourself exponent, can create a sense of dignity in the most formal of paved courtyards. Whatever type of container is decided upon, however, it must have a sufficient number of drain holes in its base to prevent the roses becoming water-logged. Its depth should not be less than 12 inches on the inside and it should have an area at the soil surface sufficient to give each rose 2 square feet in which to grow. The bottom of the container should be first filled with about two inches of crocks or pebbles, about 1 inch across. On top of this, soil should then be placed, filling the pot or trough to a height, that is about 2 inches from its top, so that there is ample room left for watering. Every large pailful of this soil should have about two teaspoonfuls of bonemeal and one of hoof and horn meal added to it and thoroughly mixed in. Sometimes town dwellers have difficulty in obtaining supplies of good garden soil, in which case, a good substitute is John Innes potting compost No. 4, which is a standard product, which, if it is not procurable locally, can be ordered from suppliers further afield. Advertisements offering it can be seen regularly in the gardening press. As a guide to how much to buy, it is useful to know that 1 cwt. of John Innes potting compost No. 4 occupies a space of 2,775 cubic inches. With this knowledge, it is simple to calculate the total quantity required to fill all the containers.

There is no difficulty regarding the maintenance of roses growing in containers. It must, of course, be remembered that roses planted in the shelter of surrounding walls do not always get their full share of rain. So they require to be regularly and copiously watered. Apart from assisting their growth, this is important because it keeps their roots moist and so reducing the risk of attacks of mildew, which may occur in such a position where air circulation is likely to be restricted. Another point to remember is that, unlike when they are growing in the open, the roots of the roses are unable to spread themselves out and seek the necessary nutrients in more distant areas. This is best overcome by giving them regular doses of liquid manure and by foliar feeding. Each autumn, a few inches of the top-soil should be removed from each container and replaced with fresh John Innes potting compost No. 4, containing the same proportions of bonemeal and hoof and horn meal as were added when originally planting the roses. In order to be sure that the drainage crocks have not become clogged with fine soil, it is as well to repot the roses after a few years. Pruning is carried out in much the same way as with plants that are planted in beds.

Unfortunately growing roses in containers does not render them immune from attacks by pests and diseases. Regarding the former the task is not too formidable because, usually when growing in pots or in beds in a patio or on a terrace, the number to handle is small and they can be dealt with by handpicking or 'thumbing' i.e. squeezing the more prevalent insects, such as greenfly and caterpillars, between the thumb and first finger. Alternatively, the insects can be eliminated by spraying with a proprietary systemic insecticide (see pages 135 and 136). The diseases, mildew and blackspot, are the most common. These are controlled as usual by spraying the roses with the appropriate specific every ten to fourteen days (See pages 142, 143 and 144).

Regarding the choice of bush roses for this purpose, it has already been pointed out that the main criterion of their suitability is that they should be short-growing. Any with this specific quality in the lists on pages 30-35 can be used. A particularly good selection can be made from the hybrid tea roses, Anvil Sparks, Belle Blonde, Cleopatra, Doreen, Duke of Windsor and Konrad Adenauer. Among the floribundas the choice is greater. Excellent roses of this type are Celebration, Copper Delight, Kerry Gold, Marlena, Meteor, Petite, Radar, Summer Song, Susan, Zambra and the various varieties of Garnette roses. In addition, the use of the polyantha pompons and the miniatures in small paved areas should not be overlooked.

Up to the present time, there has been a tendency for the planting layouts for patios, terraces and courtyards always to be formal, but it is possible that the application of the more modern technique of mixed plantings of shrubs, roses and hardy perennials to island beds, made in a paved area, using the more dwarf varieties, might enable the garden-lover, whose growing space has been drastically curtailed, to enjoy on a small scale a good many of the beauties of a larger garden. While it is not appropriate to discuss this idea in great detail in these pages, it can be conceived that the giants, such as *Rosa omeiensis pteracantha*, and the species and shrub roses that feature in the mixed borders at Wisley could be substituted by hybrid tea and floribunda roses, the taller growing conifers could be replaced by dwarf species and the more vigorous-growing herbaceous plants planted towards the front of the beds by the lower growing ericas, miniature roses and dwarfer varieties of herbaceous plants. It is easy to imagine what a beautiful and satisfying effect could be obtained if this were done.

In much the same way, the shorter growing hybrid teas, floribunda, polyantha pompon and miniature roses can be effectively included in small rockeries. By using them in this way, colour can be given to rock gardens in the summer, which is a time when they can be rather dull, after the glorious display that has been put up by the spring-flowering alpines. If roses are, however, planted in rockeries, it should be remembered that it might be necessary to make pockets of suitably rich soil in which they can flourish because so many rock plants prefer rather poorer growing conditions.

CHAPTER TWENTY

Growing Roses in Pots under Glass and for Floral Decoration

Growing Roses in Pots Under Glass

Those who have a greenhouse should have no difficulty in growing roses in pots. The pleasure of having roses in full bloom with perfect flowers in May, or even April, is immeasurable.

Roses that are to be grown in pots under glass should be either already in pots by, or be potted up, in October, according to the manner in which they are initially obtained. There are several ways in which such roses can be acquired. Firstly, they can be bought in containers, especially in these days of 'instant' planting, but usually the choice of variety in this case is rather limited. Secondly, one can ask a nurseryman to recommend some varieties suitable for the purpose and then pot them. The third way is to dig up selected cultivars from the garden and put them into pots. The fourth is to buy some rugosa root stocks in the autumn and plant them in pots, and then bud them the following June with buds of the chosen varieties, after which, they are treated in exactly the same way as any other budded roses (See Chapter 21). In the October of the year following budding, they are ready to be handled in the same manner as any other potted rose. Although the last named is the best method, it will be realised that it takes longer for the rose to reach maturity when it is used.

A good growing medium for both established roses and root stocks is John Innes potting compost No. 4, to which a small amount of John Innes base fertilizer is added, or a mixture of four parts of good loam, one part of well-rotted farmyard manure or peat (plus bone-meal) and one part of coarse sand, into which is incorporated a proprietary rose fertilizer at the maker's recommended level. Eight-inch pots should be used initially, but the more vigorous varieties might require re-potting into 10 inch pots a few years later. Good drainage in each must be ensured by placing a good layer of crocks at the bottom.

The potted roses are brought into the greenhouse in November, where they are kept without water until the end of December or early January, when they are hard pruned to two eyes from the base, after removing all sappy weak and crowded shoots, to prevent them becoming leggy. In subsequent years, the old wood should be first removed together with any weak shoots and the well-ripened growths cut back to three or four buds. At the time of pruning, the roses should be given one watering and then left until new shoots appear, after which they should be watered regularly, but not more than once a week.

At this stage, it is likely that a little heat will have to be provided to protect them from frost. Usually it is sufficient to place an oil burner in the greenhouse or to switch on a short length of electrical tubular heating, if it is installed in the greenhouse. It must, however, be remembered that roses are not hothouse plants and they must not be forced unduly. The best way of controlling the heat at the correct level, is to aim at keeping the temperature in the greenhouse between January and April at that which might be expected to be reached out of doors two months later, i.e. during the period March to June. As a guide, these temperatures are of the order of 60°F maximum during the day, falling to 45°F at night during January and February, 65°F and 55°F respectively in March and 70°F and 60°F respectively in April. During the latter month, temperature control can be quite tricky and in some years it is necessary to use shading on the roof and top side glass to prevent scorching. During the whole period careful attention must be given to the top ventilators to secure a movement of air so that the risk of mildew is minimised. Draughts, and these might be caused by indiscriminate use of the side ventilation, must be avoided.

During April, for certain in May, the roses will commence to bloom, producing flowers that are more superior in quality than anything that is normally obtained from trees growing in the open because they have been carefully tended and protected against bad weather.

After the roses have either been cut for cut-flowers, or have faded and have been dead-headed, the pots are put out into the open in June, preferably in a position where there is some shade during the day. For the next few months they need little attention except watering when it is very dry and the removal of any buds that may form. In October, an inch or so of the top-soil should be removed from the pots and they should be re-filled with John Innes potting compost No. 4 or the potting mixture already described, to which a little bonemeal and a handful of dried well-rotted cow manure is added, prior to their being re-housed in November.

Fortunately, roses grown under glass are reasonably free from pests and diseases. Generally, a daily spraying with clean water will remove any greenfly or similar insects. Caterpillars are best removed by hand-picking. Red spider mite is sometimes a danger, but this can be extirpated by spraying with a white oil preparation (See page 136). Sometimes mildew attacks potted roses. This is dealt with by spraying with the appropriate fungicide (See page 143). Black spot is a rarity and rust never seems to appear on indoor-grown roses.

A SELECTION OF ROSES FOR GROWING UNDER GLASS

Hybrid Tea Roses		Floribunda Roses	
Colour	*Variety*	*Colour*	*Variety*
White	Message	White	Iceberg
Blue/Lilac	Sterling Silver	Blue/Lilac	Lilac Charm
Yellow	Golden Melody	Yellow	Allgold
	Spek's Yellow	Coppery Yellow	Copper Delight
Deep Orange/		Yellow/Pink/	
Reddish	Mojave	Salmon	Circus
Pink/Silver	Gavotte	Pink/Silver	Daily Sketch
	Rose Gaujard	Salmon Pink	Dearest
Salmon Pink	Femina	Salmon/Light	
Deep Pink	Ballet	Red	Spartan
Vermilion	Baccara	Carmine Pink	Paddy
	Fragrant Cloud		McGredy
Deep Red	Karl Herbst	Crimson	Red Wonder
		Vermilion	Flamenco
		Various	Garnette Roses
			(See pages
			32 and 33.)

Roses for Floral Decoration

It is only the intention in these pages to indicate some of the varieties of roses that are particularly good for floral arrangements. No attempt is being made to discuss the art of arranging flowers.

There are certain basic requirements that merit a rose as being regarded as satisfactory for this purpose. The principal ones are having long stems, few thorns, buds that are comparatively slow in opening and blooms that hold their shape, retain their colour and last fresh in water for a long time. There are some varieties of roses that possess all these qualities to a great degree. They can either be grown under glass or in the open. The thing that determines whether they are to be grown indoors or outdoors is the time of the year at which the blooms are required. Also, there are some roses, more particularly shrub roses, that are valuable to flower arrangers because, in addition to providing very beautiful blossoms, they give very attractive foliage of various hues and beautifully shaped, coloured fruits in the autumn. Perhaps most treasured of all roses for floral decorations are the Garnette roses, which are really floribundas. They have camellia-shaped blooms with a wide range of colours that includes red, pink, rose-salmon, yellow, white, orange and apricot. They all have an outstanding ability to remain fresh for a long time when cut and placed in water. It should, however, be mentioned that gardeners in some districts have difficulty in growing them outdoors. Since this is by no means universal, readers are advised to plant only one or two in the first instance and see how they flourish for a year or so. If they are not successful in their location, they must grow them in a greenhouse, if they wish to have this type of rose for cutting.

In the accompanying table, a selection of roses that are excellent for floral decoration is given. The particular varieties that are more usually favoured by florists are indicated with an asterisk (*).

A SELECTION OF ROSES FOR FLORAL DECORATION

Hybrid Tea Roses		Floribunda Roses	
Colour	*Variety*	*Colour*	*Variety*
White	Youki San	White	Iceberg
Blue/Lilac	Intermezzo		Ice White
Yellow	King's	Ivory White	Ivory Fashion
	Ransom	Creamy Peach	Chanelle
Apricot Yellow	Dr A. J.	Blue/Lilac	Lilac Charm
	Verhage*	Yellow	Allgold

Hybrid Tea Roses		*Floribunda Roses*	
Colour	*Variety*	*Colour*	*Variety*
Coffee Brown	Fantan	Orange/Apricot	Shepherd's Delight
Orange Amber	Apricot Silk		
Pink	Pink Favourite	Orange	Orangeade
Red and Gold	Katharine Pechtold*	Pink	Queen Elizabeth
Deep Salmon		Red	Red Favourite
Red	Montezuma*	Vermilion	Flamenco
	New Yorker*	Various	The Garnette Roses*
Vermilion	Baccara		(See pages 32 and 33.)
	Interflora*		

CHAPTER TWENTY-ONE

Propagation 1 – from Cuttings and by Budding

There are three ways in which roses can be propagated, viz. (a) by planting seeds; (b) by taking cuttings, and (c) by budding. The first method of propagating roses is not used in practice, except in the very special case of hybridization, when a new species or variety is created, because in the first place, seedlings of garden roses rarely survive the rigours of their first winter unless they are cosseted in the very rigidly controlled conditions that are maintained in a rose breeder's greenhouse. In the second place, garden roses are never grown from seed because any particular variety cannot be reproduced by this method. When a seedling does reach maturity, it is very different in character from its parents. This is due to the very complex pedigree, that is possessed by modern roses.

Roses can be grown true to type by taking cuttings and rooting them. This method, however, is more applicable to the vigorous floribundas of the Poulsen type and ramblers than to hybrid tea roses. Even with the former types, experienced rosarians know that cuttings of the yellow varieties do not readily root and that reds and pinks are rather more amenable to this method of propagation. Two disadvantages of growing roses from cuttings are firstly that it takes very much longer to obtain mature roses than is the case when they are budded; and secondly, the resulting plants are sometimes weaker in constitution because the roots that develop are not so vigorous as those of the species, that are normally used as rootstocks in budding. On the other hand, as the roses, that are raised from cuttings, are growing on their own roots, there is no risk of suckers.

There are, however, occasions when it is necessary to propagate roses by taking cuttings. A case in point is that of miniature roses, which are reproduced in this way (and sometimes by root-division), because when they are budded on to rootstocks they grow much larger, and, in consequence, lose much of their loveliness. In addition, plants produced by this latter method often have a much shorter life.

When taking cuttings, it is imperative to select well-ripened

A Good Exhibition Hybrid Tea Rose
Peer Gynt. Yellow.
Raised by Kordes, 1968

Good Exhibition Floribunda Rose
hur Bell. Golden Yellow.
sed by McGredy, 1965

Hybridization. Transferring the pollen from the male parent, the floribunda rose, King Arthur, to the stigma of the female parent, the hybrid tea rose, Prima Ballerina, at the Nurseries of R. Harkness and Sons Ltd., Hitchin, Herts.

shoots because generally soft sappy wood will not readily grow roots. Growers vary in their views on the best time to take cuttings. This varies from August to November. This variance probably means that there is a pretty good chance of success at any time during this period. September is regarded as a particularly good time because there is still some warmth in the soil and it has not become too wet. Cuttings, which initially should be about 12 inches long, are taken by cutting a selected shoot about $\frac{1}{4}$ inch below an eye, using secateurs. It is then trimmed up at this end with a horizontal cut immediately below this bud, using a sharp knife. It is then cut to a length of about 10 inches with a cut, that slopes downwards away from, and just above, a bud higher up the stalk in the same way as is done when pruning. Next all the leaves are removed except the top two or three. Each of the eyes, that is likely to be beneath the ground, is eliminated by means of a wedged-shaped cut. This minimises the risk of suckers growing. (Fig. 23). At the bottom of a wedge-shaped trench, about 9 inches deep, which has been previously dug, is placed a layer, three inches deep, of a mixture of sand and peat in equal parts. The cuttings are then inserted into this, with a distance of 4 to 6 inches between them. After this, the soil is filled into the trench and gently trodden in so that the cuttings are standing upright. If desired, the bottom end of each cutting may be dipped in water and then into a hormone rooting powder, removing any surplus by gently tapping before planting. This assists rooting. This is not, however, essential for success, if the cuttings are put into the planting mixture mentioned above and the soil is suitable for growing roses. Real success in rooting any cuttings lies in being sure that they are planted with $\frac{2}{3}$ to $\frac{3}{4}$ of their total length below the ground. This assures that there is no likelihood of any movement occurring and this assists the rapid formation of the roots.

The cuttings are allowed to remain in this position until the following autumn. They can then be dug up. Although not all will have taken, quite a number will have rooted. These can then be planted out in their permanent beds.

Propagating Roses by Budding

Because of the limitations already discussed of propagating roses from seeds and cuttings, it has become the universal practice to increase them by firmly attaching buds of the cultivars that are to be

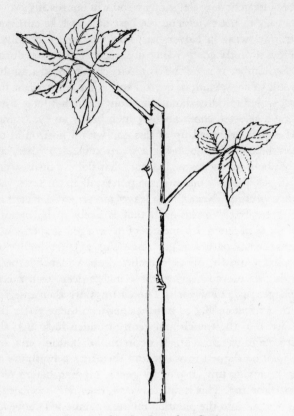

FIG. 23. *Growing Roses from Cuttings*

All the leaves except the top two or three are removed. Each eye that is
likely to be beneath the ground is cut out

raised, to the stem of a related member of the rose family, which is
well developed on its own root system. If the union between the
tissues of these two individual plants is mechanically sound, the
living cells of the rose cultivar will continue to divide and the normal
process of growth will continue. This process, which is to be described in greater detail below, is known as *budding*.

Before going further, consideration must be given to the partner
of the union that provides the roots through which the combination
feeds. This is known as a *rootstock* or *understock*. The actual species or

cultivars of the rose family that are employed vary throughout the world according to the climatic and soil conditions. The most common rootstock used by rose hybridists in the United Kingdom is *Rosa canina* (dog rose or briar). Unfortunately there are a large number of sub-varieties, cuttings of which are erratic in growth, differ in their ability to root and often have a strong tendency to throw suckers. For this reason, amateur hybridists would be ill-advised to take cuttings from a dog rose flourishing in a hedgerow for the purpose of producing rootstocks. It is very important to have a reliable one. This can be provided by a sub-variety of *R. canina*, *R. canina laxa*, which is very uniform, does not throw suckers and has a high take. It is highly recommended in cases where there is heavy or average soil. On poor, sandy soil, *R. multiflora* is a more suitable understock. It is also known as '*polyantha simplex*' or '*simplex*'. Both the above-mentioned types are normally used for bush roses, but in the case of standards either *R. canina laxa* or *R. rugosa* are most favoured.

There are two alternative methods of obtaining rootstocks. The first is to grow them from cuttings of any of the recommended types. This is done in the autumn in exactly the same way as with garden roses, which has already been discussed, except that with *R. canina laxa*, it is an advantage to use always a hormone rooting compound to accelerate rooting. When they are rooted in the following March, they are dug up and planted in a nursery bed, about 10 inches apart, in rows 2 feet 6 inches apart. Their roots should be placed in the soil as shallow as possible. For the convenience of the budder later on (See page 197), the root stocks should be planted so that they are sloping towards the spot where he will stand when he is ultimately budding.

As an alternative to growing rootstocks from cuttings, it is possible to buy seedling stocks from certain nurserymen, who specialise in them. It is claimed by some experts that roses budded on to such stocks have a longer life than those grown on cutting stocks. These seedlings are planted in February or March in a nursery bed in rows in exactly the same way as described for rooted cuttings. As with them, they are put in at an angle to the ground. There is, however, one difference that should be noted. In the case of seedling rootstocks, they are planted with that portion of their main stems between the fork of their roots and the lowest green shoot above, i.e. the *neck*, about 1 inch above the level of the soil. After being planted, the soil must be earthed up round the neck so that the bark is maintained in a moist condition.

Although there are some exhibitors, who plant their cuttings in their permanent quarters and bud them in these beds, it is generally thought to be inadvisable to do this. This means that readers, who are keen on budding must experiment to some extent to ascertain which procedure suits their purpose best. It is claimed by some rosarians that the best blooms are produced on maidens or during the early life of a rose tree. It could therefore be that it is more convenient to proceed in this way when producing exhibition roses because the interest in them becomes lessened as they become older. In the case of roses, however, for garden display the objective must be to produce strong hardy roses that will yield plenty of blooms for many years to come. In such a case, it is important therefore to be sure that a healthy vigorous growing bush is established. In consequence, for this purpose, it is recommended that the rootstocks are first planted in a nursery bed and transplanted to their permanent quarters after they have bloomed for the first time. This allows the roots to be pruned to encourage the development of a strong root system. It also gives an opportunity to cull the weaklings which inevitably appear.

Equipment Required for Budding

The first essential is a razor-sharp, good quality, budding knife, which has a wedge-shaped end to its handle, which is used for lifting the bark. For tying in the buds, either good quality raffia or plastic tape, cut into lengths of about 2 feet, is needed. As an alternative, there are available nowadays specially made rubber patches with metal fasteners. These have the advantages of being more easily fixed, expanding to allow for the swelling of the bud and rotting readily.

The Time to Bud Roses

The best time to bud is on a day following rain, when the atmosphere is humid during July and August. In the absence of rain, the ground should be watered copiously during the previous 24 hours.

Budding Bush Roses

Budding is by no means a difficult task and is one that can be soon mastered by an amateur. The principle is the same for all types of roses. The various stages are outlined in the following paragraphs:

(1) A good healthy shoot bearing a bloom of the variety to be budded, that has just faded, is ear-marked, but not cut right away, because it is far better to prepare the rootstock first and apply the bud fresh.

(2) Next, a suitable rootstock is selected. This should not have a diameter greater than $\frac{1}{2}$ inch at the neck because if greater, the bud and rootstock tissue may not knit together satisfactorily. Also the healing of the cut when the latter is headed back (See page 200), may be slow and infection might set in. The heaped up soil on the selected stock is then removed to expose the neck, which is thoroughly cleaned with a well-wetted cloth. This is a very important step because the presence of dirt seriously impedes the joining up of the two components.

(3) The green shoots, that have grown on the rootstock are next pressed down towards the ground by the breeder placing his knee on them so as to give good access to the neck. It is to facilitate this action that the rootstocks are set at an angle to the ground when planting. Using the budding knife, a cross cut, about $\frac{1}{4}$ inch long, is next made horizontally on the neck at a distance of about 1 inch above the fork of the roots. This cut should be quite shallow, only reaching just below the depth of the bark. Starting about $\frac{3}{4}$ inch below this cut, an upright shallow incision is made to form a T with the first one. At the finish of this upward cut, the corner of the bark is just lifted by a twisting movement of the knife. The bark is then raised along the whole length of the vertical slit by inserting the wedge-shaped end of the budding knife under the bark. This must be done with great care so that it is not damaged in any way. The rootstock is now ready to receive the eye (See Fig. 24a).

(4) Without any delay the selected rose shoot is cut. All the thorns are removed and the leaf stalks trimmed back to a length of $\frac{1}{2}$ inch. This remaining portion is of considerable help when inserting the buds into the T incision on the rootstock. The shoot is then held in the left hand and the middle buds, which are invariably at the right stage of development, are cut out. This is done by inserting the budding knife, which is kept continuously sharpened during this operation, into the shoot at a point about $\frac{1}{2}$ inch above an eye, cutting it out with a downward movement which ends just behind the bark at the same distance below it, keeping the cut away portion no thicker than is necessary to remove the bud (See Fig. 25).

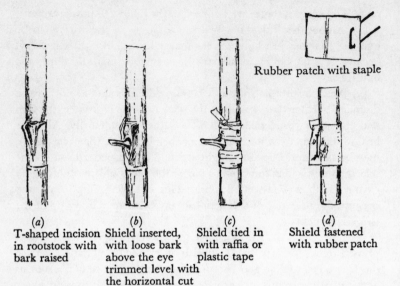

Rubber patch with staple

(a)
T-shaped incision
in rootstock with
bark raised

(b)
Shield inserted,
with loose bark
above the eye
trimmed level with
the horizontal cut
in the rootstock

(c)
Shield tied in
with raffia or
plastic tape

(d)
Shield fastened
with rubber patch

FIG. 24. *Budding Roses*

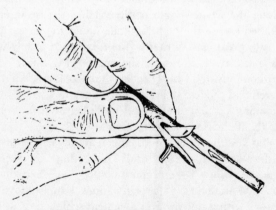

FIG. 25. *Budding Roses*

Cutting out the bud

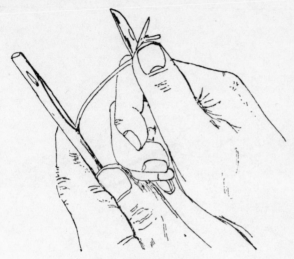

FIG. 26. *Budding Roses*

The loosened eye is torn gently away from the shoot so that a thin strip
of the bark remains attached to it

The loosened eye is then torn gently away from the shoot so that a
thin strip of the bark remains attached to it (See Fig. 26). The
separated bud, if properly taken, will have a sliver of wood at the
back of it. This is exposed by pulling down the bark and it is removed by snatching it out with a brisk, but gentle, twisting action.
Care must be taken to see that the bud itself is not torn out with the
wood when this is done (See Fig. 27).

(5) The piece of bark containing the eye, which is called the
shield, is next trimmed so that the part below the bud is ½ inch long
and wedge-shaped (See Fig. 28).

(6) Holding it by the remaining ½ inch of the leaf stalk, the trimmed shield is fitted in the T-incision, with the wedge-shaped
extremity at the bottom, and the bark of the rootstock is pressed
back over it. The loose bark above the eye is then cut off level with
the horizontal cut in the understock. (See Fig. 24b). If the bud is to
be fixed with a rubber patch, the remaining portion of the leaf stalk
is carefully cut away without disturbing it and the rubber stretched

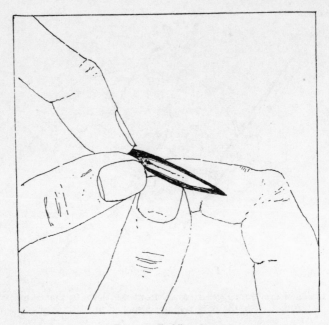

FIG. 27. *Budding Roses*

To separate the bark containing the eye from the sliver of wood behind it, the attached long strip of bark is pulled down and the wood is snatched out with a gentle twisting action. Care must be taken to ensure that the bud is not torn out with it

across the eye and round the neck of the understock to the back. where it is firmly fastened by means of the metal staple (See Fig. 24d). If raffia or plastic tape is used, the bud is firmly tied in by making two turns below and three above it. In this case, the small remaining piece of leaf stalk need not be removed as it does not interfere in any way with the fastening of the bud (See Fig. 24c). When left, in fact, it dies in about 3 weeks, signalling that the bud has taken.

(7) Nothing further is done until the following late January or early February, when, if the weather is dry and frost-free, all the top growth on the rootstock is cut away at a point 1 inch above the bud. This action is known as *heading back* (See Fig. 29).

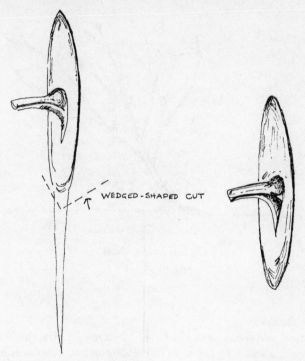

WEDGED-SHAPED CUT

FIG. 28. *Budding Roses*

An untrimmed
shield

A shield ready for
insertion in T-cut
in the stock

(8) Roses budded on to *multiflora* stocks are liable to be wrenched out by the high winds. This can be prevented by supporting the new shoot with a short thin stake inserted in the ground, placed close to the opposite side of the rootstock to the bud and running parallel to it, and two moderately tight ties, one just below and the other just above the eye.

(9) The budded stocks are allowed to remain in the nursery bed until after they have bloomed in the following summer. From October onwards, they are transplanted to their permanent quarters. At the time this is done, the roots are pruned back, particularly the deep penetrating ones, in order to induce a good growth of fibrous surface roots.

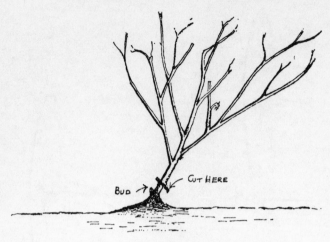

FIG. 29. *Budding Roses*

Heading Back

Budding Standards

For this purpose, rootstocks have, of course, a straight vertical stem, some 2 feet 6 inches high in the case of half standards and 3 feet 6 inches to 4 feet in that of standards. The rootstocks are either briar or *R. rugosa*. The method of budding employed is similar to that already described, but in the case of the former stock, the budding is done on two or three laterals as close to the main stem as possible, whereas with rugosa, two or three buds are usually put in on opposite sides of the stem itself. If raffia ties are used on standards, they have to be cut away after the first month or so, when the bud seems to have become set, unlike dwarf varieties, on which they can be allowed to rot during the winter. Again, as with bushes, the standards are headed back in the following January or February, and similarly moved to their permanent quarters in October of the same year after flowering for the first time in the summer.

CHAPTER TWENTY-TWO

Propagation 2 – By Hybridization

There is no doubt that there are many keen gardeners who wish that they could breed a completely new rose variety. Unfortunately, while it is a task that can be undertaken by anybody who has a greenhouse with a little heat, many have neither the time nor the patience to achieve this objective. Nevertheless the propagation of roses by hybridization is a subject in which a lot of gardeners sooner or later get interested, and, even if they cannot undertake it, no doubt, they might like to know how it is done. It will be appreciated that all the early hybrids were created by natural fertilization, but during the past 200 or more years it has become increasingly the established practice for man to breed new varieties under strictly controlled conditions. While many very excellent new roses have been introduced by this means, there is little doubt that there has been a fairly large element of chance in their production. There is nowadays, however, more work being carried out that has a very definite object, such as breeding disease-resistant cultivars, less vigorous roses, 'blue' roses and so on. To carry out hybridization successfully, particularly, when it is being done with a specific objective in view, breeders must have an appreciable knowledge of the pedigrees of possible parents and to be acquainted with principles of plant reproduction. The latter subject is dealt with in Chapter 23.

In this chapter, it is proposed to deal with the practical aspects of rose breeding. For this purpose, however, it is necessary for the reader to become familiar with the structure of the rose's reproduction organs. Referring to Fig. 30, the male organ, which is known as the *stamen*, is composed of the *anther*, which produces the male sex cells or pollen grains and the *stalk* or *filament* by which it is attached to the rest of the flower. As will be appreciated from the illustration, a rose bloom has a number of such stamens. When the pollen grains are ripe, the anther bursts and they are released. They are usually covered with a heavy covering of wax to protect them against the bad weather. The female organ, the *gynaecium*, is composed of a number of *carpels* or *pistils*. Each of the latter are made up of three

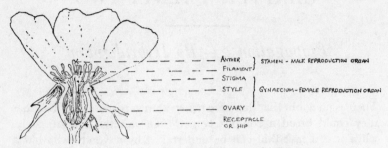

FIG. 30. *The Reproduction Organs of a Rose*

parts. At the uppermost end is the *stigma*, which becomes sticky, when the *ovule* is ripe and the flower is ready to be fertilized. The stigma is joined by a tube-like *style* to the *ovary*, which is the swollen basal part of the carpel. This contains the ovules. The ovary in the case of a rose is firmly attached to the inner wall of the *receptacle* or hip, which is the enlarged top of the flower stalk. When a pollen grain falls on the receptive stigma, it is stimulated to grow a pollen tube, which passes through the style into the ovary, where it fuses itself on to an ovule and fertilization takes place. There are three main ways in which the pollen grains can reach the receptive stigma – (1) by dropping from the anthers in the same flower, when the process is termed self-pollination; (2) from the anthers of other plants through the agency of insects, animals, wind, etc., or (3) by being deliberately planted there by a rose hybridist.

When breeding a new variety, it is the object of the hybridist to select parents that have the desirable characteristics, either in themselves or their ancestors and to bring the male reproductive cells of one into contact with the female ones of the other in the hope that at least one of resulting progeny will show a marked improvement on its forebears. This is done under strictly controlled conditions so that there is no risk of pollen from other roses being transferred by insects or the wind. It is the usual practice to plant the prospective plants in pots during the autumn and to house them in a cool greenhouse in January or February, when they are pruned and allowed to flower not earlier than April or May. By this date some bright warm days, which are conducive to pollination, are likely. On the day that the rose, which is destined to be the female parent, i.e. the one in which the ovules are to be fertilized, is due to open, all its petals except the five outside ones are removed. This should be done carefully so that no pieces are allowed to remain as these may lead to botrytis, which is a disease that is caused by a fungus, *Botrytis cinerea*, which is particularly active on damaged plant tissues.

Next the anthers are removed by cutting through the filaments at their base with a pair of scissors. This operation is known as *emasculation* (See Fig. 31). About a day later the stigma normally becomes shiny and sticky, showing that it is prepared to receive the pollen from the male parent. All, but the outside petals, are removed from the latter to expose its stamens. The pollen grains are then transferred on to the stigma of the female by means of the finger, a camel hair brush, or rough textured cloth or, perhaps best of all, by applying the anthers of the male parent directly to it (See photograph opposite page 193). The stalk of the fertilized rose is then labelled with a record of its parents, its reference number and other relevant information.

Some weeks later, it will be noticed that the remaining petals fade and fall off, and the seed pod swells. This is usually an indication

FIG. 31. *Hybridization*

Before Emasculation   After Emasculation

that fertilization has taken place. The receptacles are allowed to remain on the plants until autumn or when the first frost arrives. They are then cut off with a few inches of stalk being retained. Care must be taken to ensure that they remain labelled so that they can be identified. They are left until December for the hips to ripen and the seeds set, storing them in a moist place.

The receptacles are cut open when they are ripe and the seeds removed. The latter are sown in pots or other suitable containers. Preferably the yield from any one crossing should be confined to a specific pot or pots so that there is no likelihood of any confusion later. The best growing medium is John Innes Potting Compost No. 1. They should be placed 1½ inches apart on the surface of the soil and pressed gently into it so that when they are covered with a sprinkling of the compost and finally with a layer of coarse sand, they are about 2 inches deep. They are next well-watered, using a watering can with a fine rose, and then placed in a cool greenhouse. There is no satisfactory way of deciding whether a seed will germinate. One must just wait and see. Usually, if the potted seeds are maintained at a temperature of 43°F, many will germinate in the following February. After this has happened the temperature is raised to 59°F. In the case of yellow roses, particularly those that have *Rosa foetida* in their ancestry, however, germination rarely occurs before the spring, 12 months' later. In consequence, no seeds that have not germinated should be discarded until a year or more has passed.

When the seedlings bloom in the summer their qualities are assessed for the first time. Any unsuitable varieties are destroyed at this stage and the remainder are allowed to grow on to about August when they would be about 4 inches high. At this point, up to four buds are taken from each of these tiny bushes and they are budded on to root-stocks in the manner already described in Chapter 21. When the budded seedlings grow and flower in the following year, they are judged again. Any varieties that look as if they might be winners are budded again in August of that year. It is usual to take on this occasion up to 50 buds of each new cultivar. In the following year, the hybridist makes his final judgement as to whether he has created a variety that has a good potential. If such is the case, it is the normal course for him to submit plants of it to the Royal National Rose Society, who will keep them under the strictest surveillance for three years at their Trial Ground at St

Albans. After this period, any that qualify will receive an award.

From this account, it can be seen that creating a new rose variety is no easy task. Seven or more years can elapse before even the best can become a commercial proposition. Although not wishing to be discouraging, it is thought that would-be rose breeders should know that the world-famous German rose breeder, Wilhelm Kordes, has estimated from his 40 or more years' observation and examination in rose trial gardens, that only 1 in 3,000 seedlings will ever reach the market. Nevertheless, what a great reward in terms of satisfaction it must be to raise an entirely new rose!

CHAPTER TWENTY-THREE

How Roses Grow and Multiply

In these days of more scientific plant breeding, it is necessary for hybridists to have some knowledge of the fundamental structure of plant tissues and the mechanism of the processes that take place when there is growth and multiplication in a plant. This is of course is a vast subject and there is only room for a brief and comparatively simple outline of it in a book of this kind.

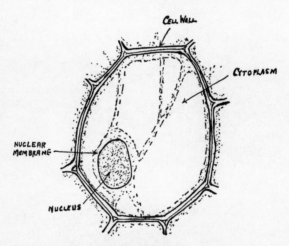

FIG. 32. *A Plant Cell*

All living tissue, both animal and vegetable, is composed of cells, (See Fig. 32), each of which has two principal parts, the living *protoplasm*, which when present in a cell is called *cytoplasm*, and an inert fairly elastic cell wall, which completely encloses the former. Within the cytoplasm, there is, among other things, a very important spherical organ which is called the *nucleus*. This is surrounded by a *nuclear membrane*. This body and its constituents play a vital part in the processes of cell division, which are essential to the growth and reproduction of plants. The nucleus contains a number of characteristic thread-shaped bodies, *chromosomes*, so named because they can absorb dye and then can be seen under the microscope. These have in turn in their molecular structure, chemical groups that are known as *genes*. These appear as nodules along their length, and in consequence chromosomes were in former days likened to strings of beads. It is through these genes that various hereditary qualities are imparted to ensuing generations by means of sexual reproduction. It is said that there are over 1000 genes in roses, which cover among many others, such important characteristics as colour, scent, vigour, freedom, and otherwise, from disease, resistance to bad weather, remontancy.

Reproduction in Plants

Reproduction in plants may take place in two ways. One is vegetative growth, or asexual reproduction, which is located in specific areas, known as the *meristematic regions*, of the plants, which are generally the tips and sides of the stems and roots. It arises from the process of cell division, in which a cell on reaching maturity divides to form two others, which are identical with itself. By this means it is only possible to reproduce tissue of the same type as that of the existing plant. No new varieties are created in this way. The other type of reproduction is *sexual reproduction*, which is brought about by special *sex cells* or *gametes* that are set apart in the organism for the purpose of producing new individuals, which might have characteristics widely different from those of their parents. These cells are male or female. In sexual reproduction, gametes of opposite sexes are fused together. Although it is necessary for them to appreciate the mechanics of vegetative growth, it is in this last process that rose breeders are particularly interested.

It has already been mentioned that the nucleus of a cell contains a certain number of chromosomes. For a reason that will be more obvious later on (see page 212), they always exist in sets of pairs in asexual cells. The basic number of these pairs in each set is always the same for a specific species. For the rose species, the chromosomes number, as it is called, is 7, i.e. the nucleus of its cells contain 7 pairs of, or 14 individual, chromosomes.

So that the processes involved in reproduction can be better understood, at this point a number of important definitions are given. Cells that contain the number of pairs of chromosomes, that is basic for any particular species, are said to be *diploid*. Because of anomalies that arise in the reaction, sometimes tissue is produced that is made up of cells that contain sets of chromosomes in two pairs instead of one, i.e. each cell contains, in the case of a rose with such tissue, 28 chromosomes instead of 14, i.e. (the chromosome number, $7 \times 2 \times 2$). Such cells are termed *tetraploid*. As is explained on page 215, it is possible to have cells in which the number is of a still higher order. Actually the cells of both hybrid tea and floribunda roses are tetraploid.

Now the important difference between vegetative growth cells and gametes is that, whereas the former cells contain, when normal, the chromosome number of pairs of chromosomes, the sets in the latter are composed of *single* chromosomes, and not pairs. So the sex

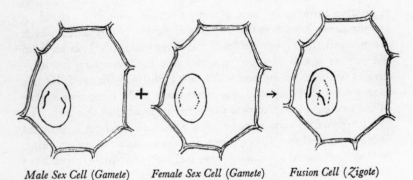

Male Sex Cell (Gamete) *Female Sex Cell (Gamete)* *Fusion Cell (Zigote)*

FIG. 33. *The Sexual Act – Syngamy*
(For simplicity, only two chromosomes are shown in each gamete)

cells contain half the number that is basic for the species, and this number is termed the haploid number. Such cells are termed *haploid*. So the vegetative growth cells of a species rose each has $7 \times 2 = 14$ chromosomes in its nucleus, whereas a gamete has only $7 \times 1 = 7$ chromosomes.

The Sexual Act

It has already been explained, on page 204, how the ovule is fertilized by the male pollen grain to form a seed that grows ulti-

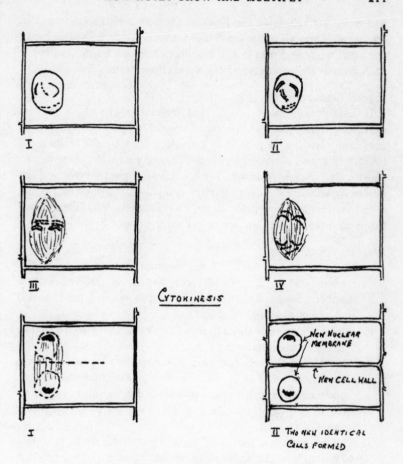

FIG. 34. *Asexual Reproduction*
Mitosis
(*For simplicity, only two chromosome pairs are shown*)

mately into an entirely new plant. Every time this takes place a male sex cell or gamete is fused together with a female one. This process is known as *syngamy*. It has already been mentioned that each sex cell contains sets of single chromosomes, and not of pairs. In consequence in a fusion cell or *zygote*, there is now the basic number of pairs of chromosomes, one half female and the other male, which will carry with them all the hereditary characteristics embodied in the genes. This cell is a normal diploid, which grows by division in the usual manner. From this, it becomes obvious why the nucleus of each growth cell contains sets of *pairs* of chromosomes (See Fig. 33).

Asexual Reproduction (See Fig. 34).

It has already been stated that vegetable growth or *asexual reproduction* takes place in the meristematic regions, i.e. the growth areas, of plants, and that it is brought about by the division of mature cells into two identical ones. This process takes place in two phases, viz., the *mitosis* in which the nucleus is split into two and the *cytokinesis*, which is the division of the cytoplasm and the laying down of the new cell wall between the two newly formed nuclei. The various stages in these two actions are described in greater detail below.

Phase 1   Mitosis
1. The confused network of chromosomes which exists in the nucleus just before cell division begins, is resolved into a number of separate threads. These shorten and thicken and each assumes a distinct shape.
2. Each chromosome thread splits lengthwise into two like parts, which are called *chromatids*.
3. The double threads continue to contract. They each gather across the equator of the nucleus. At the same time the nuclear membrane disappears and a spindle of delicate fibres begins to form in the cytoplasm from points or poles at the top and bottom of the cell.
4. The longitudinal halves of each chromosome separates and each daughter chromosome moves to opposing poles by means of the spindle. This process, which results in equal division of the chromatic material of the original nucleus, is known as the *anaphase*. Following this the chromosomes at each end of the cell once again become a tangled network. The spindle becomes less conspicuous and nucleus membrane reforms. This stage, which is called the *telophase*, marks the end of the mitosis or the division of the nucleus.

Phase 2 Cytokinesis
1. Between the two new nuclei, a new cell wall begins to form.
2. The original cell is divided into two identical, but smaller, ones, by the formation of a new cell wall.

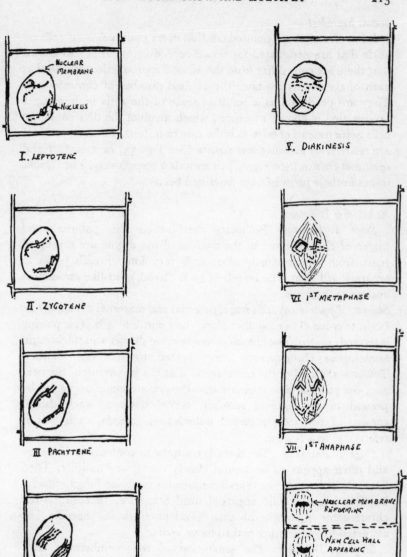

FIG. 35. *Sexual Reproduction (Meiosis)*
Reductional Division
(For simplicity, only two chromosome pairs are shown)

Sexual Reproduction

It has already been pointed out that every plant has some cells set aside that are designated for sexual reproduction. It is also known that these sex cells differ from the asexual reproduction cells in that each of them only contains the haploid number of chromosomes. They are produced as a result of some of the cells undergoing a process that is known as *meiosis*, which involves the division of the cells twice instead of once as is the case in mitosis. These two actions are referred to as *reductional division* (See Fig. 35) or meiosis 1 and *equational division* (See Fig. 36) or meiosis 2 respectively. The various stages in these processes are described below:—

Reductional Division

Stage 1. *Leptotene* Following fertilization the paternal and maternal chromosomes in the nucleus of the zygote are a tangled mass, from which shortly afterwards very long threads begin to separate. All along the length of each thread bead-like *chromomeres* appear at intervals.

Stage 2. *Zygotene* At this stage, paternal and maternal chromosomes begin to come closer together along their entire length. This pairing is termed *synapsis*. The chromosomes become shorter and thicker and homologous chromomeres are attracted towards one another. Towards the end of the last stage and at the beginning of the next one, the pairing is so intimate that the chromosomes appear to be present in the haploid number. Since, however, each thread consists of two closely paired homologous threads, each pair is referred to as a *bivalent*.

Stage 3. *Pachytene* The threads continue to contract and thicken and often appear to be wound closely round one another. Then later, each chromosome thread commences to divide longitudinally, but this is not usually apparent until Stage IV. In addition the chromosome members of each bivalent begin to become less attracted to one another and so move apart.

Stage 4. *Diplotene* The separation of the members of each bivalent continues until they are only held together at one, or possibly two in the case of long chromosomes, points. Each such point of contact is termed a *chiasma* (plural: *chiasmata*), meaning a cross, for there is at these points an exchange or crossing over of chromatid parts.

Stage 5. *Diakinesis* The bivalents become evenly distributed around the periphery of the nucleus. The chromosomes continue to contract, becoming shorter and thicker and more regular in shape. There might also be a reduction in the number of chiasmata. The close of this stage is marked by the disappearance of the nuclear membrane and the appearance of the spindle.

Stage 6 *1st Metaphase*   The bivalents take up their positions on the spindle, which now becomes quite evident.

Stage 7. *1st Anaphase*   Each bivalent splits into two and each part (i.e. Member chromosomes) migrates to the opposite poles.

Stage 8. *1st Telophase*   In this stage the nuclear membrane may reappear and the new cell wall form to separate the two new nuclei. Although in certain organisms these last processes do not occur and the equational division is entered into right away.

It will be realised that each of these cells, that have been formed, contains a set of *pairs* of chromosomes and not a set of *single* chromosomes, the haploid number, which is the characteristic of sex cells. Further action, *equational division*, therefore must take place to divide the nucleus again. It is apparent if this does not occur the chromosome content of the cells will increase in successive generations.

Equational Division

Stage 1. *2nd Metaphase*   Within a short time the chromosomes in each new cell nucleus (or potential one), arrange themselves around the equatorial plane of the spindle that rapidly develops. The two spindles, however, are at right-angles to each other and both are at right-angles to that in Stage 6 of the reductional division.

Stage 2. *2nd Anaphase*   At the beginning the chromosomes divide into two along their length. The chromatids, so formed, move to the poles of the spindles.

Stage 3. *2nd Telophase*   The nuclear membranes reform, the spindles disappear, and cytokinesis occurs. Thus four haploid cells (sex cells or gametes) are produced from the diploid one that originally entered meiosis.

Polyploidy

It is already known that normal cells of plants are diploid, but there are organisms that have cells that contain sets of more than one pair of chromosomes, i.e. more than twice the haploid number. These are described as being *polyploid*. If, for example, sets of two

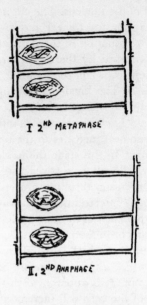

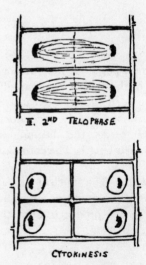

FIG. 36. *Sexual Reproduction*
Equational Division

For simplicity, only two chromosome pairs are shown

pairs (4 chromosomes) are present the cells are tetraploid. These are the type that exist in hybrid tea and floribunda roses. There are in addition cells that are triploid, i.e. containing sets of $1\frac{1}{2}$ pairs or 3 chromosomes, hexaploid (3 pairs – 6 chromosomes) and even higher.

Polyploid cells usually arise out of mechanical interferences during gamete formation resulting in sex cells that are diploid instead of haploid. If such a gamete is fertilized with a normal sex cell, a triploid one would be produced, while the fusing together of two diploid cells in the sex act would result in a tetraploid. Sometimes injury to a plant will result in the growth of shoots that are larger than normal. These are usually found to contain polyploid tissue. If, for example, tomatoes, which have diploid cells, are cut back sometimes the new growth is tetraploid.

Polyploids can also be induced in plants by treating the meristematic regions of the stems with colchicine. This alkaloid prevents the production and operation of the spindle in mitosis. In such cells, the daughter chromosomes fail to separate, resulting in a cell with a double set of chromosomes being formed. This chemical has been used to treat commercially important crops, such as cranberries, blueberries, peaches, apples, chestnuts and grapes, because the tetraploids, that are produced, yield larger fruits. As referred to in Chapter 13, it has also been applied to the buds of diploid species roses to give ones with tetraploid cells, which can then be crossed with selected hybrid tea and floribunda roses in an endeavour to breed roses that are less susceptible to black spot.

CHAPTER TWENTY-FOUR

The Future of Roses

Often books on roses include a chapter on their history. While this makes very interesting reading, the authenticity of such information is often challenged and, in any case, it is doubtful whether it is of any great value to average gardeners. It is thought better therefore to consider instead what the future holds for these lovely plants and record for the benefit of rose hybridists at least some of the qualities that seem at present to be looked for in the roses of tomorrow.

Although there is no doubt that many roses will continue to appear as a result of more or less chance breeding and of natural mutation, it seems likely that in the years to come there will be more organised hybridization programmes with well-defined objectives. This trend is already indicated by the research activities sponsored in the United States by the United States Department of Agriculture and in the United Kingdom by the Royal National Rose Society. No doubt such bodies will continue to observe the requirements of the various sectors of rose growers and plan their future work schedules as far as possible to meet these needs.

There are a number of different groups of interested parties in the rose world and it is worthwhile considering their various wishes in this respect. The largest of these, in terms of individuals, is undoubtedly the amateur gardeners. Although most of their desires are shared by others, their more urgent requirements are to have plants that are less vigorous and tall-growing than many of those that exist today so that they are more appropriate to small gardens, which have probably come to stay and cultivars that are immune from disease and resistant to the effects of rain and sun. In addition, there are some amateurs, who would like to see varieties that do not produce suckers. The latter entails carrying out more intensive studies on the rootstocks that are used for budding.

Other groups of the public sector, viz., the rose exhibitors and floral arrangers, both have their wishes regarding future roses for their own particular interests. Perhaps most prominent among those of the former are to be given varieties that habitually grow on long stems, do not produce blooms that have split or 'scrambled' centres and have sufficient number of petals to ensure their holding their shape over a long period. The flower arrangers in their turn are looking for roses that give long arching sprays of blooms and foliage, which are so much treasured in arrangements, and more blooms with peach, brown and parchment shades. The latter is a trend that has already commenced.

Turning to the commercial and professional aspects of rose-growing, it is probably not realised by everybody how important the large scale growing of roses under glass for the florist trade is becoming and how fast it is increasing in the British Isles. This development is something that could be of great benefit to gardeners and others because a good healthy industrial interest often fosters research work. It is important therefore to mention some of the qualities that this trade are likely to look for in future roses. Among them are immunity from disease, ability to produce flowers without damaged outside petals so that labour is not involved in removing them prior to marketing, and being capable of standing up to rough handling, both in packing and transit. They should also be easily and cheaply grown in large quantities under glass in the winter, when the demand is tremendous. Roses that are destined for the cut-flower trade must have a long life and have the ability to absorb water readily, so that they quickly revive after being packed for prolonged periods. Lastly, whatever might be argued elsewhere, scent could be a very important criterion of whether a rose is a good seller or not, and every endeavour should be made to include it among the characteristics of future roses that are designed to be used for this purpose. On reflection, it cannot be denied that most of the items in the above specification would satisfy almost any gardener.

There are no doubt others, but there are two remaining categories of people whose interests as far as roses are concerned are closely allied. These are the garden designers and those responsible for the layout and upkeep of our many very beautiful public gardens. Undoubtedly they subscribe fully to every wish that has already been expressed, but among those qualities in future roses, for which they would make a special plea, would be ability to withstand the rigours of the severest winters in open and exposed places and being capable of replacing comparatively low-growing annuals in formal bedding out, which under present conditions is very costly in labour. In addition, they would like to have more new cultivars that give good ground cover and roses that would flourish in the shade.

If rose breeders are successful in meeting even only a proportion of these requirements, it is conceivable that there will be changes in the form which these lovely flowers take. But does this really matter? For so long we seem to have been obsessed with the idea that a rose in its present style is the only one acceptable. The long history of this flower proves beyond doubt that whatever it is like in the future, it will still be something of exquisite beauty, just as it has always been in the past.

Index

Illustrations are denoted by page numbers in *italic*